REBEL WOMEN
OF THE WEST COAST
Their Triumphs, Tragedies and Lasting Legacies

RICH MOLE

VICTORIA · VANCOUVER · CALGARY

Heritage House Publishing Company Ltd.
#108 – 17665 66A Avenue
Surrey, BC V3S 2A7
www.heritagehouse.ca

Library and Archives Canada Cataloguing in Publication
Mole, Rich, 1946–
     Rebel women of the west coast: their triumphs, tragedies and lasting legacies / Rich Mole.

Includes bibliographical references and index.
ISBN 978-1-926613-28-4

     1. British Columbia—History. 2. Washington (State)—History. 3. Oregon—History. 4. Women—Northwest, Pacific—Biography. I. Title.

FC3811.M65 2010   971.1'0082   C2010-900171-0

Series editor: Lesley Reynolds.
Cover design: Chyla Cardinal. Interior design: Frances Hunter.
Cover photo: Library of Congress, George Grantham Bain Collection (LC-DIG-ggbain-10578).
Sections of *Waste Heritage* have been reproduced with permission of the University of Ottawa Press.

 Mixed Sources
Cert no. SW-COC-001271
© 1996 FSC
FSC

The interior of this book was printed on 100% post-consumer recycled paper, processed chlorine free and printed with vegetable-based inks.

Heritage House acknowledges the financial support for its publishing program from the Government of Canada through the Canada Book Fund (CBF), Canada Council for the Arts and the province of British Columbia through the British Columbia Arts Council and the Book Publishing Tax Credit.

 BRITISH COLUMBIA ARTS COUNCIL   Canada Council for the Arts   Conseil des Arts du Canada

13 12 11 10   1 2 3 4 5

Printed in Canada

Contents

Bethenia Owens-Adair rose from semi-literacy to become one of the West Coast's first female doctors.

Prologue

ASSISTANT SECRETARY OF STATE *Dixy Lee Ray opened the clippings file. In the spring of 1975, news stories didn't make for happy reading. On its relentless drive to the Vietnamese capital, Saigon (now Ho Chi Minh City), the North Vietnamese Army had overrun Hué, Chu Lai and Da Nang, all in the previous few days. Most American forces had already pulled out; only Marines and civilians were left and—what was this?*

A small item, easily overlooked: the North Vietnamese were closing in on the little town of Da Lat and a South Vietnamese nuclear facility the US had helped build. A few minutes later, Dixy had shoved aside everything she had on her agenda. The danger was clear: a working nuclear facility could fall into the hands of the enemy. However, this issue was outside her jurisdiction. Dutifully, she called an appropriate contact at the Department of Energy, but the person was out of touch, skiing in Colorado.

To hell with protocol! Dixy called the Department of Defense directly, urging the military to fly in, snatch the plant's fuel rods and destroy the installation. Soon the mission was accomplished, without casualties. But what if she hadn't bothered to read the bulletins?

This seat-of-your-pants stuff was driving her crazy, and it was more evidence that she was working with a bunch of sycophantic, platitude-mumbling bureaucrats in what she called "the most unmanaged department in the federal government."

Rebel scientist Dixy Lee Ray was sick of it.

Introduction

REBEL: A PERSON WHO RESISTS any authority, control or tradition.

Traditional beliefs, along with social norms and conventional wisdom, change over time, often as a result of the actions of people we still call rebels. Here are amazing stories of singularly courageous women—driven, obsessed, sometimes desperate women whose nonconformist beliefs, attitudes and, most of all, actions, made them rebels in society's eyes. If their attitudes and behaviour seem less rebellious to us than they did to their contemporaries, it is because these women *did* rebel and effected the changes we take for granted.

"I always tell girls that they can do anything they want to

if they only want to enough," Atomic Energy Commissioner Dixy Lee Ray once counselled. If that sounds easy, thank women such as Dixy, who in the early 1950s was the University of Washington's first and only female faculty member in zoology or botany. To surmount chauvinistic attitudes, a young woman who wanted a career outside of teaching, nursing or secretarial work needed more than desire. She needed to have nerves of steel and a will of iron.

Unorthodox male behaviour was, and still is, tolerated and even lauded as get-up-and-go, grit, perseverance and novel thinking. Not so in women. Female perseverance is still too often regarded as stubbornness, and novel thinking is judged irrational, an attitude carried over from an era when "intelligent" women knew that "their place" was at home with their children. Their place was not in managerial offices, university lecture halls, broadcast studios, polling booths, government assemblies or operating theatres. In *Rebel Women of the West Coast*, you will meet women who asked only for equality and respect in all of these "forbidden" places.

In June 2009, an Alberta Member of the Legislative Assembly (MLA) blogged his female staff and constituents, "Men are attracted to smiles, so smile and don't give me that 'treated equal' stuff; if you want equal it comes in little packages at Starbucks."

There is little likelihood that the need for rebel women will disappear any time soon.

1

Rebels of the Trail

WHAT MOVES PEOPLE TO GIVE up their livelihood, abandon habit, leave homes and loved ones and travel to far-off, hostile lands?

The reasons that compelled thousands of 19th-century Americans and British colonials to venture into the western wilderness of North America varied, depending on the time and place. A.L. Fortune, one of a tiny number of Canadians making a journey across most of the continent, explained that "for many miles deep Ontario's habitable lands were occupied," and he felt, "her sons would year after year follow me and others to the west not finding scope near home to satisfy their longings."

Thomas McMicking, leader of one Canadian exodus,

saw his decision as a part of a larger destiny. Both their present communities and any future settlements they might create "shall become one and the same country." All it took for Fortune, McMicking and their companions to make the final decision was a compelling event. By spring 1858, they had it: gold had been discovered in New Caledonia (British Columbia).

In the early 1800s, there were few women on the trail. When missionary Mary Walker ventured west before the fabled Oregon Trail existed, it was because she felt compelled to convert western Natives to Christianity. But she had to marry in order to do so. In British territory, wives were persuaded to stay home to raise children and were separated from their wandering husbands for months, years or sometimes forever. Not Catherine Schubert, who fought to accompany her husband. Thousands of women would set out later, but when Mary and Catherine left civilization behind, they were the true rebels of the trail.

Missionary Mary Walker

Mary Richardson was puzzled. Elkanah Walker, the "tall and rather awkward gentleman" introduced to her earlier that day by her family's minister, was back again. Perhaps, she guessed, he had returned to arrange details of the evening church meeting her devout Presbyterian family was hosting. Her parents invited Walker to stay the night.

Early the next morning, Mary found the man sitting

alone, reading his Bible. Nervous Mary and intense Elkanah began to talk. He said he was hoping for African missionary work. Mary had also asked for placement on the "dark continent," but because she was single, the church's board of foreign missions had turned her down. It was a bitter disappointment for someone who had decided to become a missionary when she was 10.

"I am going to surprise you," Walker blurted. "I may as well do my errand first as last. As I have no one engaged to go with me," he rushed on, "I have come with the intention of offering myself to you."

This man—a mere stranger a few hours before—was proposing marriage! And that is how Mary Richardson Walker made the most important decision of her life. But the significance of her decision didn't lie in marriage to a man she hardly knew; that was commonplace for early 19th-century women. It was accepting the condition built into that marriage: travel to a wild, little-known territory thousands of miles away. Knowing that Mary had been rejected as a missionary, the foreign missions secretary had suggested Walker meet her. A letter to Mary from a church lecturer suggested that here was a way for her to reach her personal goal and fulfill her obligation to the Lord: marry this man and do God's work with him, wherever that might take her. Had Mary lived the narrow, prescribed existence of most women of her time, she might have remained oblivious to the board's machinations. However, because perceptive

Mary was worldly as well as spiritual, she suspected she was being manipulated. She was correct.

While deeply religious, Mary's parents nevertheless had enrolled their daughter in progressive schools that offered more than basic literacy, an unusual decision in the 1830s. Consequently, as a young girl, Mary became fascinated with science and had harboured the unorthodox idea of becoming a woman doctor. However, while attending a Methodist revival meeting one night, young Mary experienced a blissful religious transformation. The fervour of that moment shaped her life and became the source of inner conflict that agonized her almost daily.

Years later, on the day of Elkanah's proposal, Mary admitted in her diary that, "The hand of Providence appeared so plain that I could not but feel that there was something like duty about it." Which would win: religious duty or her heart's desire? By evening, Mary determined that duty "must prove the path of peace."

Mary and Elkanah were married on March 5, 1838. They set off just days later to bring salvation to the Natives, travelling from Maine by buggy, stagecoach, train, steamboat and, finally, on horseback, not to Africa (tribal conflict made it too dangerous), but "through Indian country to the Columbia River," as their US passports put it. (Passports were necessary because the Walkers' destination lay outside the frontier boundaries of the US.)

The Walkers were bound for Marcus Whitman's

recently established Presbyterian mission, located in an enormous swath of wilderness called Oregon Territory, which extended up the west coast to the Queen Charlotte Islands, directly east to the Rockies and south to the border of Mexico's Spanish California. This wilderness belonged to no nation. There was no discernible path to follow. It would be two more years before the first wagon would roll over the future Oregon Trail.

The Walkers set off on horseback from Missouri with three other missionary couples, including the Grays, newly-weds like themselves. For all their pious intent, the missionaries' personalities clashed repeatedly. Less than four days out, "some of the company feel disposed to murmur against Moses," Mary recorded. "Moses" was William Gray, the group's self-appointed leader, who had already visited Oregon Territory. A month later, Mary wrote sadly, "We have a strange company of Missionaries. Scarcely one who is not intolerable on some account."

These ill-tempered missionaries were fortunate. Despite harsh conditions, they didn't starve or die of thirst and managed to keep relatively healthy. Although already pregnant, Mary bore the discomforts well, including the fact that eight disagreeable people were forced to squeeze themselves into a pair of 9-by-12-foot tents each night. Things got worse. "We were scarcely expecting rain and made no preparation. In the night it stormed tremendously. Our bed was utterly flooded. Almost everything wet. No wood, so used 'prairie coal' [buffalo dung]. I am thinking how comfortable my father's hogs are." At least this fuel was plentiful; Mary's party carefully walked their horses through herds of thousands of buffalo.

Outwardly compliant and pious, Mary suffered inner conflicts about her intolerant husband. "Should feel much better if Mr. W. would only treat me with some cordiality," she confessed. "It is so hard to please him I almost despair of ever being able to." The next day, Mary "rode twenty-one miles without alighting. Had a long bawl. Husband spoke so cross I could scarcely bear it."

But Mary couldn't hide her fascination for the vast land they travelled through. "The bluffs resemble statuary, castles, forts, as if Nature, tired of waiting the advance of civilization, had erected her own temples." Mary climbed to the top of one and chipped out a piece to add to her plant and mineral collection. (Years later, unorthodox Mary transfixed visitors with the results of her taxidermy skills.)

Elkanah seemed incapable of sharing her unladylike interests. "I wish Mr. W. would seem to feel as much interest in viewing the works of nature as I do," Mary admitted. Later, after a short absence from Elkanah, Mary said that she "was glad enough to see my husband, he seemed glad to see me. I suppose he really was, for he has no faculty of making believe."

More than five months after setting off, the Walkers and their squabbling companions reached Waiilatpu, the

Whitman mission near Fort Nez Perces (later called Fort Walla Walla), a Hudson's Bay Company (HBC) fort. Three of the couples were crammed into Whitman's former cabin. It was a tempestuous time, culminating one December day in Mary's labour. Her water broke at 5 a.m., signalling "approaching confinement." Elkanah was away again, and it was a long morning.

At almost 9 a.m., Mary noted, "I became quite sick enough—began to feel discouraged. Felt as if I almost wished I have never been married. But there was no retreating, meet it I must." At 11 a.m., "I began to be quite discouraged. I had hoped to be delivered ere then . . . But just as I supposed the worst was at hand, my ears were saluted with the cry of my child. A son was the salutation. Soon I forgot my misery in the joy of possessing a proper child."

Typically, Mary turned to the Bible to articulate her feelings. "I truely [*sic*] felt to say with Eve, I have gotten a man from the Lord. [As] with Hannah, for this child I prayed. Thanks to a kind Providence for so great & unmerited a blessing. The remainder of the day I [was] comfortable. Husband returned in the evening with a thankful heart, I trust, & plenty of kisses for me & my boy."

The Walkers were overjoyed. Their companions, the Smiths, were not. Asa Smith, who took the trouble to do the arithmetic, concluded that the baby arrived "just *2 days* over nine months from the time they were married, the 5th of March." He was clearly disgusted by the unseemly fact.

"What I think about such things, you know already. I feel thankful that I am not in such an embarrassed situation & at present there is not prospect of it."

By early fall, the Walkers and another couple, Myra and Cushing Eells, happily said goodbye to the Grays and Smiths and founded their own mission, Tshimakain, which was located a few miles northwest of the present-day city of Spokane. Elkanah decided that if the Natives were to effectively receive the word of God they would have to abandon their entire way of life. "They must be settled before they can be much enlightened," he wrote the foreign missions' commissioners. "While they retain the habit of roving . . . their children cannot be gathered into schools and instructed." Elkanah felt they must give up hunting and become "cultivators of the soil" as soon as possible.

Years after her religious conversion, Mary's rebellious spirit caused her to question her worthiness. "I have been reviewing my life . . . in what respect am I the better for having lived . . . I am just as prone as ever to indulge in vain and wicked thoughts, to forget God and the high calling with which I am called. I am still the same stupid, indifferent creature . . . What good can such a vile creature expect to do among the heathen?"

During their nine years at the mission, Mary bore and raised six children. She worked exhausting 16-hour days in and around a 14-square-foot cabin built of log walls chinked with mud. She trod a dirt floor strewn with pine needles and

16

a leaky roof of poles, grass and dirt. She cooked in a fireplace, never a stove, made soap, cultivated the garden, helped in the fields and milked the cows. She diarized her everyday travails in a series of startlingly nonchalant entries:

"Sat up all night, dipped twenty-four dozen candles."

"Cut out six pairs of shoes today."

"The potatoes freeze in the cellar. Found the house was taking fire in consequence of the chimney being heated. Had to repair it, a cold treat for so cold a day."

"This morning part of the wall of our house fell. Husband was in the room in bed when it began to fall. He escaped without being hurt much. Son's little chair was broken to pieces." And, as if that weren't bad enough, "The chimney fell with the wall and just as it fell, it began to rain."

Almost exactly four years after leaving comfortable, civilized Maine, Mary wrote, "Rose about five. Had early breakfast. Got my house work done about nine. Baked six loaves of bread. Made a kettle of mush and have now suet pudding and beef boiling. I have managed to put my clothes away and set my house in order. At nine o'clock p.m. was delivered of another son."

Plagued with doubts, ground down by toil, Mary found little comfort in her marriage. "I am tempted to exclaim, Woe is me that I am a wife. Better have lived & died a miserable old maid & none to share & thereby agrivate [*sic*] my misfortune. But it is too late. O may He who in his providence has suffered me to become a wife bless me in that relation & enable me to discharge every duty with Christian discretion & propriety."

"He," however, couldn't stop Mary from feeling herself "a grieved and disappointed wife. Disappointed, not because he is not as good as I anticipated, but," she added, in true rebel fashion, "because I have not gained that place in his heart that I fondly expected & which I think a wife ought to possess."

Newcomers arrived, bringing more than fond dreams and good intentions. They brought disease. Angered when measles decimated their people but left whites largely unharmed, Cayuse Natives concluded the sickness was a plot to destroy them all and struck back in the only way they knew how. Their 1847 attack on Whitman's mission left the leader, his wife and over a dozen followers dead. The Cayuse took others hostage, including two young children who, ironically, succumbed to measles while in captivity.

Shortly after the massacre, the Walkers closed their mission and left for the safety of the HBC's Fort Colville. On behalf of her children, Mary composed a poem to help them remember their birthplace. Stoic to the end, she gave no hint of inner doubts, frustrations or exhaustion in her verses:

Tshimakain! Oh, how fine, fruits and flowers abounding,
And the breeze, through the trees, life and health conferring.
And the rill, near the hill, with its sparkling water
Lowing herds and prancing steed round it used to gather.

And the Sabbath was so quiet and the log house chapel
Where the Indians used to gather in their robes and blankets.
Now it stands, alas forsaken: no one with the Bible
Comes to teach the tawny *skailu* (people) of *Kai-ko-len-
so-tin* (God)
Other spots on earth may be to other hearts as dear;
But not to me; the reason why, it was the place that bore me.

After nine years of effort, the Walkers did not convert a single Spokane Native to Christianity.

Overlander Catherine Schubert

Picking up the shards of crockery from the floor, Catherine Schubert knew her husband, Augustus, would be back. Despite the flying dishes, loud shouting and door slamming, he soon would shuffle back into their home-cum-grog shop for the usual mumbled reconciliation. Then the Schuberts would begin to pack up—all five of them, if Catherine had her way. There was no way Augustus was going west without his wife and children.

The incident related above was included in a book about Catherine written by an esteemed Canadian author. But did it actually occur? There is no way to know. Unlike the Walkers, the Schuberts kept no diaries, and if anyone wrote about it, those accounts have been lost. Catherine remains a woman of mystery. However, given the time, place and existing evidence, there is little doubt that the couple's marital relationship and interactions with others were tempestuous.

Antagonism and discord were commonplace in the lives of immigrant pioneers, and steadfast determination to the point of bloody-mindedness was often crucial for survival. The Schuberts survived into old age, Catherine becoming famous as the first white woman to make the life-threatening journey across 2,000 miles of hostile wilderness.

As a feisty teenager, Catherine O'Hare had escaped the potato famine in her native Ireland and eventually became a domestic servant for a wealthy Massachusetts family. Augustus Schubert had come from Germany as a stubborn, bearded 19-year-old. By the time he met Catherine, over a decade later, Augustus was an established carpenter and ready to marry. After she met Augustus, Catherine decided she was ready, too.

Back in 1856, moving west was Augustus' decision. He sold their little house and off the newlyweds went, following the advice of *New York Tribune* publisher Horace Greeley. "Go west," Greeley told his readers. For Catherine and Augustus, that meant Minnesota Territory, the very edge of civilization.

Augustus' first project was a house with an oversized front room. That was to be the Schubert tavern. It was a shrewd move. The nearby US Army post, Fort Snelling, housed many thirsty men. A few miles up the Mississippi, the little town of St. Paul was booming. Hundreds of riverboats disgorged mobs of people, and many stayed. It was likely Augustus kept swinging a hammer while

Catherine opened beer bottles and wiped the bar. She also bore children. By 1860, there were two boys and a girl.

In one way, the children were a blessing, as they helped keep Augustus put. He'd got that faraway look in his eye again. It wasn't A.L. Fortune's thoughts about encroaching civilization that caused Augustus to gaze west. It was gold. In the future west-coast colony of British Columbia, they were digging up nuggets on the Fraser River. Others in St. Paul were headed west, but the Schuberts had children to consider. Besides, business was good. Two years later, in 1860, it wasn't gold that finally prompted the Schuberts to leave. It was safety.

The newest arrival, baby James, was in his cradle when Catherine heard the sound of shattering glass. She dashed to the baby's bedroom in time to see a Sioux warrior crawling in on a plank he had laid against the windowsill. She snatched up little James and fled. Augustus grabbed a fireplace poker, rounded the house, intercepted the would-be kidnapper and laid on with a will. The next night, Augustus walked out of the beer hall to face 40 angry, shouting Sioux. Wisely, the Schuberts decided to take the threats seriously.

While Minnesota was home to fewer than 200,000 white settlers, it was also home to almost a million mostly unhappy Sioux, who repeatedly complained about broken government treaties. In 1857, a small war party had decimated the little hamlet of Spirit Lake on the Minnesota–Iowa border. Hunger stalked the Lower Sioux Indian

Reservation; a proud people were becoming desperate. Yet, treaty payments and food distribution were slow. It seemed that Spirit Lake hadn't taught the authorities anything.

A few days after the threats to life and property, the Schuberts and some of their neighbours decided to leave. They led their loaded pack horses north, up the frigid Mississippi and Red rivers. Their journey took them over 500 miles into British territory and through the imposing limestone walls of the HBC's Fort Garry. Their decision was timely; the little party escaped the Great Sioux War, which would later claim almost 500 lives.

The Schuberts thought that what worked in Minnesota would work just as well on the east bank of the Red River, opposite the fort. They built a roadhouse and tavern (locals called it a "grog shop") onto their new home. Augustus Schubert soon achieved notoriety. The Red River Settlement represented the raw frontier; many of Schubert's customers were Métis, mixed-blood buffalo hunters with fewer social skills than Fort Snelling's white soldiers. Overimbibing patrons had a habit of passing out. One night, Augustus helped well-known sot Michael Sweeny to his bed after a particularly strenuous night of elbow bending at the Schubert establishment. In the morning, Michael was discovered where Schubert had left him, stone cold dead. The story made the pages of the Red River Settlement's *Nor'Wester*.

Later, a hefty court-imposed fine of five pounds levied against the former Minnesota beer-hall proprietor made the *St. Paul Press* (although the details of Schubert's offence were not printed). To add insult to injury, Augustus returned home from the rustic courtroom to find Natives had broken into the tavern and absconded with 10 gallons of whisky and all the crockery and dishes. This would have been cause enough for a man like Schubert to pack up, but he soon had another reason: the big gold strikes now being made on BC's Cariboo creeks.

In May 1862, a newly constructed sternwheeler, *International*, swung into the current at Georgetown, Minnesota. There had been no steamer on the Red River for months. Told of *International*'s imminent arrival by the new HBC governor, who had travelled north on horseback, the Red River Settlement was ready to celebrate. The boat's sighting was signalled by cannon fire. Passengers answered with a ragged volley of musketry. Knowing what those passengers represented, there is little doubt Augustus Schubert was part of the welcoming throng.

The men walking down *International*'s gangway wouldn't tarry long in Fort Garry. They were headed for the Rocky Mountains and Cariboo gold. Augustus Schubert wasn't going to miss his chance this time. He talked to the gold seekers and planned to travel west with them. His wife and family would stay behind. However, Catherine put her foot down. She was not bringing up children, keeping house, tending the garden and pouring beer and whisky all by herself.

Thomas McMicking and future Overlanders thrashed up the Red River on the sternwheeler *International*'s maiden voyage before tying up at Fort Garry's warehouse, seen here.

HUDSON'S BAY COMPANY ARCHIVES, ARCHIVES OF MANITOBA, HBCA 1987/363-I-11/2

The wilderness was no place for women, let alone children, Augustus probably countered. Others, including educated Queenston leader Thomas McMicking, had done the "proper" thing, leaving wives and families behind. But Catherine likely didn't care about Upper Canada's social conventions, what men thought was proper or where Augustus thought a woman's place was. Catherine hadn't escaped Irish famine or Minnesota Sioux for a bleak life no better than widowhood. If Augustus wanted to leave, they would all leave. Desperate to join the trek, Augustus agreed.

The Schuberts' long route traversed what eastern

Canadians were calling "the great lone land." Extending north to the Arctic, west to the Rockies and, originally, south to what would become the states of Minnesota, North Dakota and Montana, the vast territory was operated by the HBC as an enormous fur preserve. Except for roving Native bands and a handful of HBC trading posts dotting the rolling prairies, the land north of the border was empty.

Augustus must have questioned his rebellious wife's sanity. Catherine was about to do what no other white woman had ever done: walk and ride 10 hours a day, week after week, through the untamed wilderness while looking after their children every step of the way. And she would do it while pregnant, a secret that the Schuberts intended to keep until it was too late for the Overlanders to order them back to Fort Garry.

The gold seekers purchased food, over 100 oxen and horses and 96 Red River carts, "the occasion of many a joke," according to McMicking. The Schuberts knew better than to laugh at the little two-wheeled wooden carts. Every year, hundreds of them rolled down the Red River trails and into St. Paul, heaped high with furs that Métis traders exchanged for housewares, farm implements and whisky. The pall of yellow dust raised by the screeching wooden wheels hung overhead for months.

The Schuberts decided to join the first group to leave. By the time Schubert found a buyer for his house and business and the family and farmhands were packed, the group was already on the trail. They caught up just in time for Augustus to attend the organizational meeting at which McMicking was voted captain of the 136-member party. Schubert's unexpected arrival almost certainly altered the meeting's agenda.

It was never the intention of McMicking's group to include women or children. Nevertheless, the Schuberts were made welcome. This magnanimous decision may have been made, in part, for Augustus' sake. Catherine's demand had placed him in an embarrassing situation. McMicking's group, like others that had set out since 1858, were companies of men. Expeditions of any kind were akin to military operations, offering tests of physical endurance, possible danger and, above all, close male camaraderie and companionship that could only be experienced outside the sphere and influence of women. Close to 250 Overlanders left Fort Garry in 1862. Only four were women. Catherine Schubert was the first of the four.

As expected, a quasi-military organization was agreed upon. The distance was over 3,000 miles, according to the new HBC governor, whose last post had been at Vancouver Island's Fort Victoria. Organization and discipline were essential if the Overlanders were to survive. Captains of various contingents—including Augustus, who represented Red River—formed a committee, and members agreed on a daily routine.

The camp was up at 4 a.m. An hour later, with the

command, "Every man to his ox!" the long train screeched off toward the distant mountains. At 11 a.m., the group stopped for dinner. The day's travel ended at 6 p.m. with the shout, "Camp ahead!" Carts were then drawn up side by side in a triangle, shafts outward, and the oxen tied up inside this formation, each to its own cart. The Overlanders pitched their tents outside the cart enclosure.

Week after week, the carts rolled westward, always making for the next HBC post over the horizon—Portage la Prairie, Fort Ellice, Fort Carlton, Fort Pitt. Men forded rivers with cattle, horses and oxen, crowding carts onto HBC scows and straining to keep the ropes taut to prevent carts and animals from plummeting down steep banks. During one almost unendurable stretch of 11 rain-soaked days, they shouldered carts out of sucking gumbo. Clouds of mosquitoes would "darken the air."

No travel was allowed on Sundays, making the Sabbath itself a blessing worth heartfelt thanks. As "the vast and lonely plains reverberated with the notes of our songs of praise, the mind was intuitively invited to contemplation," McMicking wrote during trailside worship. Surely, he thought, the significance of the hardy souls braving this incredible journey went beyond picking flecks of gold out of the bottom of prospectors' pans. The singing moved him to "enquire whether these sounds might be recognized as the footfalls of advancing civilization."

By the time the "toil-worn, jaded, forlorn and tattered

company" reached Fort Edmonton, "our most intimate friends at home could scarcely have recognized us," McMicking admitted. Exchanging oxen and carts for pack horses and saddles, the group headed toward the mountains. The day they left the little Catholic mission of Lac Ste. Anne, one worried Overlander "heard an Indian laugh, and exclaim in French, 'They are on the road to Hell!'"

However, weeks later, at the headwaters of the Fraser River, most of the five-month journey had been completed without the loss of a single member, and no wagon-train attack had occurred. In fact, as McMicking later stated, they took "red men of the prairies to be our best friends . . . before we reached the end . . . we were only too glad to meet with them." The Natives gave them food, including salmon and huckleberry cakes, and later, badger, beaver and bear.

Nevertheless, starvation threatened the Overlanders during much of their journey, and emaciated animals were abandoned and sometimes eaten. The party split up, with 36 people, including the Schuberts, travelling overland to the North Thompson River on their way to the HBC's Fort Kamloops. McMicking and others took their chances on the Fraser River. Giving them canoes, Natives murmured, "Poor white men no more," correctly predicting that some would die in the rapids.

We know much of the Overlanders' ordeals. Three people kept journals, three published newspaper accounts and re are a few letters. However, we know little of Catherine's personal trials on the trail, simply because none of these writers thought to include them in their accounts. "Who can tell what she endured?" asks Margaret McNaughton, 19th-century author and wife of a later Overlander. "No doubt her heart often quailed, but with true motherly instinct she would forget her own sufferings in protecting and comforting her children."

McNaughton's reference to "true motherly instinct" was typical 1890s sentiment, but we have no evidence to refute it. Decades later, snatches of Catherine's conversations with family and friends were recalled. Notes were taken while Catherine's elderly son, James, reminisced about events he experienced as a two-year-old, but could not possibly have remembered first-hand. The rest is conjecture. Historians apparently never talked at length with the Schuberts before their deaths early in the 20th century.

We know Catherine rode horseback more than she walked, with a child tucked into a large basket suspended on either side of her saddle. Sometimes the men hoisted a Schubert youngster on their shoulders as they forded streams or climbed hillsides. One man remembered Catherine kindly doing his laundry when she did her family's wash. Like all wives and mothers, she cooked and scrubbed while comforting, scolding and encouraging her family.

Mile after exhausting mile, Catherine trudged on, over grasslands, through swamps and forests and up and down narrow mountainside ledges so dangerous that "a single blunder, one false step" meant "instant destruction," McMicking recorded. Finally, Catherine rafted down the Thompson River, no doubt hugging her children close as the foam flew and the wooden platform heaved and shuddered beneath her.

In mid-October, they beached their raft on the riverbank opposite Fort Kamloops. Two days later, Catherine winced in pain. Details of these, her most critical moments, are still in dispute. However, the daughter-in-law of the child born that day recalled Catherine's own version of events. Frantic with concern, Augustus ran downriver to a nearby Native camp for help. There, the confused, frightened women didn't understand his gestures and shouts. Augustus dashed back to the raft and helped Catherine deliver their new baby himself, shocking the other men in the party. Somehow— aided, no doubt, by voluminous clothing—Catherine had managed to keep her pregnancy a secret. The news spread quickly. Curious Native women came to see and stayed to help care for mother and newborn. The baby girl was christened Rosa, in memory, it was said, of the rosehips Catherine gathered to stave off her children's hunger.

Thomas McMicking and a few others managed to visit the gold creeks for a few days. Most didn't even do that. Like others, McMicking turned his back on dreams of riches and trekked to the coast, where he was later reunited with his family. Of all the thousands of pounds of provisions and supplies the group packed across the prairies and mountains, the only unnecessary items, McMicking confessed, were mining tools.

Augustus Schubert found work as an HBC carpenter and cook, but gold fever still held him in its grip. Catherine had left Fort Garry to be with her husband, but, nevertheless, they remained separated for many years as Augustus searched in vain for his big gold strike. Meanwhile, Catherine operated inns and, later, a domestic-science boarding school near Kamloops.

None of the Overlanders would ever forget their journey, and many would also remember Mrs. Schubert's subtle effect on them all. "The kindly sympathy of many of our men was frequently manifested to the heroic woman and her small children," one recalled. "Her presence in the company helped to cultivate a kindly and more manly treatment of man to man."

In his philosophical tribute, Thomas McMicking told newspaper readers that Catherine "exemplified the nature and power of that maternal affection which prompts a mother to neglect her own comfort for the well being of her child." But McMicking had merely described most mothers. He came closer to defining Catherine's unique and rebellious spirit when he wrote, "Mrs. Schubert has accomplished a task to which but few women are equal; and, with the additional care of three small children, one which but few *men* would have the courage to undertake."

2

Ballot-Box Rebel:
Abigail Scott Duniway

ABIGAIL DUNIWAY WAS PLUCKING DUCKS behind the house when the visitor rode up. She barely gave her husband and the newcomer a glance as they talked. Abigail was frantically busy, as she had been every day since her wedding.

In spite of having less than a year's formal education, Miss Abigail Scott had become a teacher in one of Oregon's few schools. Obviously, she owed her career to the frontier environment rather than her credentials. She discovered that she was in the right place at the right time for matrimony, too. Men vastly outnumbered the few available white women. A comely 18-year-old "intellectual," Abigail quickly became very popular.

The man she chose was good-natured Ben Duniway,

a young rancher who, coincidentally, had left Illinois for Oregon two years before Abigail's own family had set out from the state on the 2,000-mile Oregon Trail. After that, Abigail's future—like that of most 19th-century women—was preordained. She immediately became pregnant.

After two and a half "weary years" living in a cabin on their first hardscrabble property in Oregon's Clackamas County, slender, sharp-eyed Abigail was the mother of two, the second child born after a labour she described as "a season of indescribable suffering." The hemorrhaging lasted hours. More children followed relentlessly. Endless physical toil replaced Abigail's teaching duties, which social mores dictated married women give up. Six years after her wedding, Abigail had already endured more suffering than most modern women experience in a lifetime.

A tornado and hailstorm in the mid-1850s destroyed everything, from barn to crops. After cowering in a corner as the twister ripped off the cabin roof, Abigail grabbed her toddler and struggled desperately for more than a mile to her in-laws' cabin. Neighbours helped rebuild the Duniway home, but three years later it burned down. If times were easier in their second "Sunny Hillside" farm, it was because Abigail—a young married woman already defying social convention—returned to teaching, "for groceries, and to pay taxes or keep up . . . horseshoeing, plow-sharpening and harness-mending."

On the morning Ben received his visitor, Abigail had her

eyes on the duck in her hand, but cocked an ear to the men's conversation. The man was asking Ben to be a guarantor on his loans. Ben led him into the house. A moment later, Abigail paused. If Ben became responsible for those debts, it would ruin them. She threw down the duck and dashed inside. She peered over Ben's shoulder. "My dear, are you quite certain about what you are doing?" she asked quietly.

The friend "looked daggers at me," Duniway recalled, but as he signed the third and last note, Ben told her casually, "Mama, you needn't worry; you'll always be protected and provided for." Ben's decision forged his wife's destiny and her struggle to win Oregon women the right to vote.

Within two years of that fateful day, crops failed and a flood carried off the Duniway's warehouse and the harvest it held. Then, the visitor defaulted on his loans. The sheriff handed the summons to Abigail. "When that obligation was made," she recalled cynically, "I was my husband's silent partner—a legal nonentity—with no voice or power for self-protection under the sun; but when penalty accrued, I was his legal representative." To pay the debt, the Duniways were forced to sell the farm.

Ben became a teamster, but misfortune clung to him like a burr. A runaway team knocked him beneath the wheels of a wagon, leaving him a semi-invalid. Abigail, the breadwinner, quickly established a private girls' school, renovating the attic of their Lafayette home to board students. She was up at 3 a.m. "to do a day's work before school time."

Nevertheless, "my work was rest for both mind and body. Health improved and hope revived."

Contributing to the *Oregon Farmer* had helped Abigail through the exhausting farm years, as she anonymously poured out her frustration and despair in letters signed "A Farmer's Wife." When Abigail advocated hired help, not for the farmer, but for his underappreciated and unpaid wife, one male reader accused her of a "vulgar, abusive tirade."

Then, Abigail turned novelist. *Captain Gray's Company*, the territory's first commercially printed novel, was not a book for upper-class ladies, but one that Abigail intended "the world's workers . . . shall read with benefit." Duniway wrote to instruct and inspire women readers through novels that were largely autobiographical. Fictional Ada, an independent-thinking Oregon Trail pioneer, shared many of Duniway's qualities. Ada "was wild!" readers were told, "because she would ape nobody's manners, was blithe and frank in her conversation with those of the opposite as well as her own sex, fearless in maintaining her own opinions."

In 1869, Abigail bore her sixth and last child. In an era of primitive frontier medicine, the pregnancy left her crippled for the rest of her life, suffering chronic pain from an obstructed bladder and prolapsed uterus, common afflictions at the time. If she feared and avoided sexual intercourse (something she never admitted), Abigail was just one of thousands of women who did so.

By the early 1860s, the Duniways were living in Albany,

where Abigail converted her second private school into a millinery and notions store. As they chose hats and sewing supplies, women welcomed the opportunity to confide their despair to the sympathetic shopkeeper: a wife's butter money was appropriated by her husband to buy a racehorse; another's husband sold the family furniture and abandoned his family; a fellow milliner had her stock confiscated to pay her husband's debt, incurred before she married him.

As Abigail listened to the heartbreak and hardship caused by insensitive and abusive men, one thing was clear to her: women's lives had to change, and change would only come with the power to strike down discriminatory laws. That power came through suffrage—the right to vote. To attain suffrage, "conventional wisdom" must be exposed as injustice. That meant changing people's attitudes.

When on buying expeditions for her store, Abigail met some compelling California suffragists and volunteered to become Oregon's representative at a San Francisco suffrage convention. Abigail was also reading *Revolution*, co-published by America's leading suffragist, Susan B. Anthony. Abigail felt Oregon needed its own suffrage newspaper.

In 1871, Abigail expanded her millinery business in Portland. Oregon's largest city was the centre of genteel urban society, and that society abhorred unseemly suffrage. "I am told that you [suffragists] have that horrid woman, a Mrs. Duniway," a stranger once confided to Abigail herself, "who drinks and smokes and swears like a man."

In this hotbed of anti-suffrage feeling, Abigail Duniway set up a press and typesetting equipment in the second storey of their new home. In the inaugural issue of her *New Northwest*, Abigail told readers her journal would be "not a woman's rights, but a Human Rights organ." She also saw her journal as a vehicle for her instructional fiction. A story's intent was often telegraphed by its title: "The Husband's Triumph"; "Her Lot, or How She Was Protected"; "Dux: A Maiden Who Dared."

"Men often utterly break down under the wheel of misfortune," Abigail wrote in *Judith Reid*, her first serialized novel, "whereas women bend and writhe under the same trials, yet come out in the end master of the adverse situation."

Having mastered much adversity, Abigail simply fictionalized chapters of her own life story: Judith Reid's husband, John, co-signs a debt; a flood destroys the warehouse that contains their crops; the loans are called, and the Reids lose the farm. Judith is the one who receives the sheriff's summons and returns to teaching to keep the family solvent. Who is regarded as the root cause of it all? Judith! "Such misfortunates are sure to come when women step out of their sphere," one of Abigail's characters huffs.

Abigail also remembered her childbirth agony. "Scream after scream pierced the smoke-laden air of the lonely cabin," she wrote in *Ellen Dowd, the Farmer's Wife*. Recalling her mother's anguished disappointment at the birth of yet another girl, Abigail has her dying fictional mother rave, "It would be a lord's blessing if it would never see daylight. Take it from me or I'll kill it!"

For 16 years, Abigail's stories depicted demeaning and seldom acknowledged gender inequities, as shown in this passage from *Edna and John: A Romance of Idaho Flat*:

> "John," said Edna, one day, after a vain effort to rise from her bed to attend to the demands of her business that had resulted in a relapse, "Couldn't you learn to make the pies and doughnuts, and carry on the business until I get well again?"
>
> "Do you take me for a woman?" John replied, with a maudlin laugh.
>
> "Then what are we to do, John? I've worn out my strength in your service, and am no longer able to carry on the work. Do you intend to let us starve?"
>
> John could not comprehend the situation. As long as there was a meal ahead he was as happy as the day.

In *Judge Dunson's Secret*, Abigail created a spirited exchange modelled after one she may have heard at a Portland convention she attended:

> "Will the lady kindly tell us what business her husband follows?" asked the presiding officer, with a merry twinkle in her eyes.
>
> "He keeps a restaurant," was the prompt reply.
>
> "What do you do in the restaurant, if the question is not impertinent?"

"I keep the books, wait at table, and wash dishes, ma'am."

A general laugh ran through the hall.

"You're your husband's partner, then?" asked the chair.

"Yes, ma'am."

"Do you share the profits of the business?"

"No, ma'am."

"Then you're a servant without wages, like the rest of us."

Leaving siblings and children to crank out *New Northwest*, Abigail embarked on her first suffrage lecture circuit in 1871. She invited Susan B. Anthony to join her for two months in the wilds of the Pacific territories. The two women travelled by wagon, on horseback and canoe. Scandalously, they spoke in a hall behind a saloon, in hotels both fine and dreadful, and from a platform at the Oregon State Fair, where Anthony commanded an audience of 1,000. The reactions to the two women's message of equality ranged from curious fascination to outright vehemence. As they made their way through the rain-drenched semi-wilderness, they were denounced by many churchmen from their pulpits. They were splattered with eggs in Jacksonville, Oregon, where a sheriff escorted Abigail through the streets to guarantee her safety. One Puget Sound woman made the mistake of inviting Abigail and Susan to her home. When he walked in, her husband ordered his wife's guests back to their wretched hotel.

In conservative Victoria, BC, where the two spoke before more men than women, it appeared Canadian gentlemen regarded the concept of women voters more distastefully than did Americans. (The following year, a suffrage bill introduced in the provincial legislature was defeated. It took BC women another 45 years to win the right to vote.)

Exhausted, Susan B. Anthony gratefully returned to eastern civilization. Abigail, however, seemed energized by the rough-hewn frontier environment. Her emotional harangues, plainly and often wittily delivered from platform and podium, were frequently more effective than the highly polished oratory of more cultured presenters.

Like the weekly production of *New Northwest*, suffrage became a Duniway family affair, with Abigail's sisters and nieces espousing the cause of suffrage associations throughout the Pacific Northwest. Brother Harvey Scott was the exception. As editor of the Portland *Oregonian*, Harvey was everything Ben Duniway was not: respected, admired and affluent. He was also something Abigail was not, but always aspired to be—a polished writer.

Harvey had rejected his sister's early, awkward editorial submission when it failed to measure up to his own impeccable prose. The episode became more grist for Abigail's literary mill: "You will never earn your salt as a writer. Making bonnets is your forte," a fictitious brother-editor sniffs in another *New Northwest* serialization.

When Harvey's *Oregonian* criticized the suffrage

movement, he elevated the antagonism between himself and Abigail beyond mere sibling rivalry. Abigail could not abide anyone who stood in the way of women's rights, no matter how well reasoned his arguments. Harvey Scott, she told her readers in 1874, had become "the meanest enemy of woman's suffrage that the state possesses today." This private split soon had disastrous public consequences. The *Oregonian* was the most influential journal of its day; many other editors looked to Scott for leadership.

Like most 21st-century media, 19th-century newspapers reported but rarely "made" the news. Stories reflected social norms. The overriding 19th-century social norm was that men controlled the press and virtually everything else. What men said and thought was on the front page and every other page. What women said and thought didn't count for much. Consequently, getting the suffrage story out was a huge challenge. The last thing suffragists needed was a large group of women making that challenge even more difficult. However, in 1874, that is exactly what happened.

Propriety, conformity and sentimental piety: that was 19th-century America's social trinity. At the very time when suffragists were desperate for legal and social change, an overwhelming number of clergymen preached Biblical literalism and warned against change, especially the changes in science that diverged from accepted Biblical teachings. It was Darwin's *Origin of Species*, reprinted for a sixth time in 1872, which acted as a lightning rod for both supporters and detractors. When Abigail editorialized, "Everybody's God must necessarily differ from every other person's God. He is the creation of the individual's mind," even suffrage supporters accused her of blasphemy.

Fear found its expression through the zealotry of the women's temperance movement. In their fight to outlaw alcohol, prohibitionists were aided and abetted by evangelical clergymen. Fanatical prohibitionists also decried suffrage, which promoted change—unseemly, distasteful and perhaps even dangerous change.

Quick-tempered Abigail lashed out at upper-class temperance women. She reminded her readers that these snobbish hypocrites who "turned with timid horror from the possible publicity and vulgarities involved in woman's voting," didn't consider it "too public to kneel in the open street, amid a half-jeering rabble, and tell Jesus the story of their sorrows, or too vulgar to enter the vilest liquor den and bandy words with degraded sots."

Mudslinging aside, there were important principles at stake. Legal prohibition of liquor was the antithesis of the freedom suffrage promoted: freedom of choice. Abigail considered alcoholism a disease, and one could not legislate an end to illness; it had to be cured. No, suffragists and prohibitionists could never unite. Moreover, pragmatic Abigail also knew the two militant groups *must* never unite.

Suffragists desperately needed the support of lawmakers in the legislature. Many of these men liked to drink or made their livelihood as hop growers, distillers, brewers, liquor distributors and saloon owners. Men might laugh at suffrage, but they hated temperance. Men might fear that if women got the vote, they would outlaw liquor.

While Abigail attended the 1884 eastern convention as a new vice-president of the National Woman Suffrage Association, Oregon prohibitionists did an abrupt about-face. The Woman's Christian Temperance Union suddenly organized its own suffrage campaign to battle whisky. Then, the *Oregonian* launched an anti-suffrage campaign. Abigail was stung by what she considered a betrayal by both prohibitionists and her brother Harvey.

When women in Washington Territory won voting rights in late 1883, it was to be a bittersweet victory. Two years later, Washington's supreme court struck down suffrage on a technicality, and women were barred from the polls once again.

In 1886, physically sick, exhausted by the battles she had waged against her foes and mourning her daughter's death from consumption, an embittered Abigail Duniway took her friends' advice and stepped away from her battle. She sold *New Northwest* and bought an Idaho ranch. But rest soon turned to restlessness. Abigail left Ben behind and took up the fray again as the acknowledged grande dame of western suffrage, lecturing, writing and quick to answer a plea for help. The road to equality travelled by Abigail Duniway was arduous and exceptionally lengthy. Her patience and endurance on that road marked her as a woman obsessed.

By 1906, the rivalry between the venerable *Oregonian* and the aggressive young *Oregon Journal* had intensified. Even then—and in spite of visits of infamous eastern suffragists—Harvey Scott remained reluctant to give that year's strident suffrage campaign its due, printing fewer and shorter stories than the *Journal* and tucking them into inside pages. In spite of lecture tours, conventions, demonstrations and six statewide referenda on the question, the *Oregonian* only grudgingly deemed suffrage newsworthy.

A more clear-sighted newspaperman than Abigail's brother would have acknowledged the momentum building in the west; the dream of women at the ballot box was becoming a reality. In 1896, Idaho had given women the right to vote. In 1910, Washington Territory followed suit. In November 1912, the governor of Oregon signed the Equal Suffrage Proclamation, written by Abigail herself. Recovering from pneumonia and blood poisoning, Abigail had directed the state's suffrage campaign from her bed. Ironically, the obvious weakness of the aging but still tempestuous leader helped accomplish what her youthful, energetic forcefulness had not: consolidating suffrage leadership and swaying public opinion.

In October 1915, Abigail Duniway, the first Oregon woman to enter a polling booth, turned to her son at her bedside and murmured, "I'm ready to go."

3

Rebel Doctor:
Bethenia Owens-Adair

LITTLE GEORGIE WAS WAILING AGAIN. That meant trouble; Bethenia could see it in her husband's tense face and clenched fists. If the baby didn't stop crying, LeGrand would explode in yet another terrifying tantrum. Through it all, his young wife had been slow to complain.

Fourteen-year-old Bethenia Owens hadn't complained when her parents had arranged her marriage to childhood acquaintance LeGrand Hill four years before. Their other decisions had turned out well ("Your father could make money faster than any man I ever saw," a customs official told Bethenia), and Tom and Sarah Owens were confident about their daughter's marriage.

A boisterous rough-and-tumble tomboy just a few years

before, Bethenia now struggled to play the dutiful wife. She didn't complain when idle LeGrand didn't finish their little house before winter (even after her father had paid for most of the materials), forcing them to cook and eat inside their first home next door, a leaky 12-by-14-foot log cabin. She didn't complain when layabout LeGrand earned nothing to pay the mortgage, although he was "handy with tools and could have had work at good wages as a carpenter." She didn't complain when he convinced her they should move in with his aunt in Yreka, California, while he tried in vain to make his fortune.

Aunt Kelly was "a real money-maker," Bethenia discovered, but one with "a husband who wheedled it out of her about as fast as she made it." She quickly set Bethenia straight: "LeGrand will just fool around all his life and never accomplish anything." Aunt Kelly did more than share her insight; she shared her success, employing Bethenia as a seamstress-in-training. She paid Bethenia directly rather than "give it to LeGrand to fool away" in some ill-advised scheme, such as the recently failed brick-manufacturing business.

Broke again by the fall of 1857, the couple moved back near Bethenia's parents' home in Roseburg, Oregon. Bethenia didn't complain—until LeGrand's shouting turned to slaps and punches. It took more than a little domestic discord to worry Sarah Owens, the Kentucky woman who had braved the Oregon Trail with her husband and little children, but now Sarah urged her daughter to leave LeGrand, saying, "With his temper he is liable to kill you at any time." Emboldened by desperation, Sarah and Bethenia agreed there was only one solution: divorce. At the time, divorce was socially unacceptable; divorcees were often shunned and their families shamed. Bethenia's weeping father could not bear the social stigma. Give the marriage another try, Tom Owens pleaded. Reluctantly, Bethenia agreed, but soon wished she hadn't.

As LeGrand's hand lashed out, Bethenia reeled. Snatching Georgie from her arms, LeGrand whipped the screeching baby unmercifully, hurled him onto the bed and then stomped out of the house.

"Broken in spirit and in health," Bethenia fled to her parents. Her father hired one of the state's best lawyers, future governor Stephen Chadwick. Bethenia sought a divorce, custody of George and restoration of her maiden name. Despite the prevailing social attitudes, Chadwick won it all, as well as court costs and the couple's livestock.

Barely able to read and write, 19-year-old Bethenia decided that she needed education to start her new life. While her health recovered, she accepted her parents' assistance, but not their money, a decision that helped heal her badly bruised self-esteem.

"I sought work in all honourable directions," she recalled proudly, taking in washing, picking and selling raspberries and mastering the first sewing machine in town. Like Abigail Duniway, Bethenia would become a teacher in spite of her lack of education, preparing new lessons each night so her students "never suspected my incompetence."

Driven to achieve, Bethenia pursued success with a single-mindedness bordering on obsession. By age 21, Bethenia was still trying to catch up. "Words can never express my humiliation at having to recite with children of from eight to 14 years of age," she remembered. Living now with little Georgie in Astoria (and still taking in ironing and washing to meet expenses), Bethenia was soon enrolled in the school's most advanced classes. Her rapid progress wasn't due to superior intelligence, she explained, but to "sheer determination, industry and perseverance" that had her lighting the lamp at 4 a.m. for pre-dawn studies before Georgie awoke and they both set off for school.

Others, including well-known Columbia riverboat captain A.C. Farnsworth, were aware of her efforts. Farnsworth offered financial assistance, with no strings attached; Bethenia could enroll in any American school she wished. "If you say so, I will not ever write to you," he vowed. But he also told her, "You are a great deal too independent for your own good. I am a good deal older than you are, and know vastly more about the world than you do."

The captain's remarks revealed he understood a lot less about his would-be beneficiary than he supposed. It was a tragic error. Bethenia wasn't about to be beholden to any man, especially one who thought he knew better than she did. Was she not good enough, strong enough, to reach her objectives on her own? The erosion of her self-confidence was too steep a price for this independent-minded single mother to pay. She tearfully declined the offer of the "thoroughly disgusted" captain. Bethenia's decision subjected her to years of penny-pinching drudgery.

By the mid-1860s, Bethenia had finally earned her teacher's certificate and contracted the construction of her first home. She taught at Bruceport's tough little Oysterville school, where, not one to spare the rod, she unhesitatingly strapped a muscular boy to set an example to his willful classmates.

One night there was a knock on Bethenia's door. To her amazement, there stood LeGrand Hill. Although he had never "offered to contribute one dollar for his child's support," he had come to ask Bethenia to remarry him. "But alas for him!" Bethenia remembered. The "young, inexperienced mother-child" who he once called wife had disappeared. Instead, Hill faced "a full-grown, self-reliant, self-supporting woman who could look upon him only with pity."

Bethenia closed the door on Hill and also on her unhappy past life. Yet, her new life as a teacher—and her modest salary—left her wanting more. Try millinery, Bethenia's brother-in-law suggested when she visited family in Roseburg. While tenants in her Astoria home kept some cash coming in, Bethenia, like Abigail Duniway, established a hat shop, one of the few acceptable businesses for a woman to own. After Bethenia had enjoyed two years of success, an aggressive and experienced competitor moved in—right next door. The only way for Bethenia to beat this new threat was, once again, through education. She left to master her craft in San Francisco, the fashion centre of the West Coast. Bethenia studied everything from hat manufacturing to wholesale operations, learning how skilled women fashioned 50 cents' worth of raw materials into beautiful hats costing up to six dollars. Back home, Bethenia had a show window installed in her small store to display her clever handiwork and staged a grand opening.

Bethenia took enormous satisfaction in providing George with higher education, a valuable advantage in life that few others enjoyed. By 1870, business was good enough to enroll George at the University of California. "I have never been so happy in all my life . . . because I have got such a good and dutiful son, who is willing to do anything his mother asks of him," she wrote. George's future seemed quite clear to his mother. "Georgie, I have a grand scheme in view for you, and if I succeed your fortune will be easily made," she hinted at one point. What we might see today as meddling was regarded in the 19th century as laudable and caring parental behaviour.

Bethenia's never-ending quest for independent success and achievement kept mother and son apart for years at a time. But Bethenia was careful to remind him, "I must not neglect my [millinery] business, for that would be neglecting you, and that I shall never do."

On at least one occasion when her young son shared his own accomplishment, his "mama" somehow managed to take credit for it: "Oh, how glad I am to hear of your success, darling! Only study hard, and you shall have every advantage. I know I shall be able to give you an accomplished education . . . all the reward I ask is to see you a great and noble man."

As he sought praise from her, she also sought praise from him. "I have made ninety-five dollars and fifty cents," she wrote a few years later, when establishing a medical practice, "enough to pay all my expenses and get all my instruments and quite a little stock of medicine. Now, darling, what do you think of that for your Mama?"

George travelled to Berkeley, California, and later, Portland, Oregon, where Bethenia arranged that he board with Abigail Duniway, who put him to work at *New Northwest*. Separated constantly from his driven, unorthodox mother, it's doubtful that the good and dutiful teenager put much stock in his mama's assertion that "without you my life would be a burden." The Christmas present of five dollars Bethenia sent that year (about $600 in today's money) was still poor compensation for their long separation.

Quite soon, Bethenia's real "burden" would become George himself. "All your letters have been short, written in a hurry and always closed by saying you have not time to write. Now how can I feel over this, George? Am I not toiling hard to make you a great man and is this the way for you to repay me?" It was little wonder that George wrote less frequently than his mother wanted. Then, perhaps in desperation, George told his mother he was going to burn all her letters.

Bethenia was "very much hurt" by his shocking confession. "Why should you wish to destroy your mother's letters, my child?" Seemingly oblivious to her son's feelings, she told him to save them all and instructed him how to do so. "I wish you to ... number all your letters, tie them all up neatly in packages and lay them carefully away."

By 1873, the warm glow of Bethenia's millinery success was fading, and she began to wonder what she could turn her restive spirit to next. Over the years, friends and neighbours had come to Bethenia in times of injury and illness. She seemed to have a certain knack for treating patients and comforting their loved ones. What if she could obtain some kind of medical education? It was an outrageous idea.

One evening, a desperate mother pleaded for her help. Standing beside the little girl's bed, Bethenia watched Dr. Palmer fumble with what Bethenia referred to euphemistically as an "instrument" (likely a catheter). Clumsy Palmer lacerated his little patient badly. The exasperated physician stepped back and began to clean his glasses.

"Let me try, Doctor," Bethenia ventured. Without waiting for a response, she picked up the instrument and "passed it with perfect ease, bringing immediate relief to the tortured child."

While the girl's sobbing mother threw her arms around

Bethenia's neck in relief, the outraged Palmer loudly berated Bethenia for her interference. *He* was the doctor in this room, not her! The incident taught Bethenia two lessons: first, her latent skills possibly went far beyond a mere knack; and, second, medical professionals—and many others— would probably oppose any attempt she made to legitimize those skills. Bethenia also knew the ranks of the opposition would likely include members of her own family.

Not all medical professionals were outraged at her growing obsession. One friendly doctor secretly lent Bethenia a copy of *Gray's Anatomy* to study at her leisure. The more she read, the more convinced she became that medicine— not teaching or millinery—was her destiny. Bethenia asked her younger sister to run her business and told her family she was off to Philadelphia to study medicine. The family, including George, was predictably aghast at Bethenia's disgraceful behaviour. Acquaintances sneered and laughed.

"Well, this beats all!" one "friend" exclaimed when she came to say goodbye. "I always did think you were a smart woman, but you must have lost your senses and gone stark crazy to leave such a business as you have and run off on such a wild goose chase as this."

"You will change your mind when I come back a physician," Bethenia joked, "and charge you more than I ever have for your hats and bonnets."

"Not much!" her customer snapped. "You are a good milliner, but I will never have a woman doctor about me!"

But there was some support, too. "Go ahead," Stephen Chadwick, now Washington's Secretary of State, told her. "It is in you; let it come out."

Bethenia also received a wonderful letter from an old friend. "You are right in deciding that your mind was not given to you to be frittered away in frivolity," wrote Jesse Applegate, the former wagon-train captain who had led her family over the Oregon Trail 30 years before. "I was right in deciding that marriage and motherhood was not intended for you by the Creator, he designed you for a higher destiny." Perhaps Jesse was right about marriage and motherhood. Bethenia had certainly experienced a mother's heartache in her troubled long-distance relationship with her only child. And at this moment, landing a husband was the last thing on Bethenia's mind.

One dismal December night in 1873, a solitary woman climbed into an overland stagecoach. The door clicked shut, and the driver snapped the reins. Inside the swaying coach, Bethenia Owens reflected on it all—the enormity of her decision, the heavy weight of her many doubts and the unknowable challenges ahead—and wept. This long journey would not only take Roseburg's rebel milliner across a continent, but would ultimately allow her to be among the few women to penetrate the invisible social barrier that shut them out of the male-dominated profession of medicine.

Bethenia's career path led to Philadelphia's homeopathic Eclectic School of Medicine, one of the few facilities that accepted women students. One year later, she returned to Roseburg as one of Oregon's first woman doctors. This distinction alone created quite a stir, but within a week, a vengeful physician unwittingly enhanced her professional reputation. Bethenia received an invitation to join six local physicians at an elderly man's autopsy. She asked the messenger to tell the good doctors she would be along shortly. The messenger didn't realize Roseburg's first female doctor was following behind so closely. Through the closed door, Bethenia heard the great roar of laughter that greeted his announcement that she was on her way. She waited a moment or two and then opened the door. Inside were the six physicians—and dozens of snickering men about town.

A doctor asked her loudly, "Do you know the autopsy is on the genital organs?"

"No," Bethenia calmly replied, "but one part of the human body should be as sacred to the physician as another."

Stung by her self-assured, logical response, Dr. Palmer, who had hatched the plot to invite her, stepped forward. "I object to a woman being present at a male autopsy and if she remains," he thundered, "I shall retire!"

What's the difference, she asked him, between a woman attending a man's autopsy and a man attending a woman's? Before he could reply, she turned and asked the doctors to put her attendance to a vote. They voted; she stayed. But the fun wasn't over yet.

"You do not want me to do the work, do you?" Bethenia asked in surprise when someone presented her with an open instrument kit. Indeed, they did. When her deft dissection was complete, the entire room rang with applause and cheers.

"On my way home," Bethenia recalled, "the street on both sides was lined with men, women and children and each anxious to get a look at 'the woman who dared.' "

Palmer had been confident his joke would come off well because Bethenia had earned her diploma in just one year, graduating as a "bath doctor." Electrical medical baths and medicinal vapour soaks were all the rage and made for a lucrative practice, but were not held in high regard by the medical establishment. However, Palmer hadn't reckoned on Bethenia's many hours with a medical tutor, her prodigious anatomical knowledge and her natural surgical skill.

The autopsy incident was a hollow victory. The good citizens lining the street hadn't been there to cheer her on. Their hostile faces told the woman doctor what she could expect. She and her sister packed up her store and moved to Portland, where Bethenia became the operator of two businesses: a hat shop and a doctor's office.

Bethenia and 19-year-old George were reunited in Portland, but they soon parted again. "From the beginning, I had set my heart on making a physician of him," Bethenia declares in her autobiography, "and I enrolled him in the medical department of Willamette University." Whether

George wanted this or not didn't matter; off he went to Salem. At his graduation two years later, Bethenia exulted, "My life's ambition was crowned with success." However, her ambition for George was not over; she soon "established him" in a pharmacy.

Despite Jesse Applegate's thoughts on Bethenia as a mother and her own professional predilections, her maternal instincts would not be denied. When an impoverished, dying woman pleaded with her to take her 14-year-old daughter, Bethenia adopted the "puny, sickly-looking little creature." At Bethenia's urgings, "dear, good" and obviously compliant Mattie Bell eventually earned a medical degree, too. In what may have been a rebellion of her own, Mattie never chose to practise.

By 1878, Dr. Owens decided to "get legit." "I cannot afford to attach myself to the odium of the epithet 'bath doctor,' " she later told one disappointed patient who was looking for rheumatic relief. Bethenia left for "a full medical course in the old school," studying at the University of Michigan. After graduation, she embarked on a tour of Europe with son George (referred to in her memoirs as "Dr. Hill") and two other women physicians in tow. Once back in Portland, her traditional medical practice flourished. Then, in 1884, the affluent, 44-year-old doctor met a childhood acquaintance, Colonel John Adair.

To those who had the temerity to ask about matrimony, Bethenia usually responded, "I am married to my profession."

That proved to be an unsustainable ideal for someone whose "nature was super-charged," she confessed, with "sentiment, love and romance." Handsome and debonair, possessing "a happy and cheerful disposition," and being a suffrage sympathizer to boot, John Adair quickly won Bethenia over, and they married.

Did Bethenia Owens-Adair ever reflect on old Jesse Applegate's words about her suitability for marriage? The doctor never said, but during the sorrowful and demanding years that followed, it's more than likely she did. She found her dashing colonel was "usually among the clouds and rarely comes down to terra ferma [*sic*]." The dreamer and schemer persuaded his bride to sink thousands of dollars into a coastal land reclamation scheme that, Bethenia's brother ruefully remarked, "was like fighting the Pacific Ocean."

At the age of 47, Bethenia became a mother again. When her tiny three-day-old daughter died, so, for a time, did the independent spirit of the formerly ambitious woman. She was still grieving when typhus struck her down. The colonel persuaded her to return to the family farm near Astoria to regain her health. It was no rest cure. Instead, the next 11 years were the most exhausting Bethenia ever endured.

While the colonel was off investigating railway schemes and other dubious business ventures, Bethenia spent hours in the saddle tending the stock and stumbled day and night through "dense undergrowth . . . obstructed with logs and roots . . . through muddy and flooded tide-lands" tending her far-flung patients.

It was too much. "I shall soon be a cripple if I live in this wet climate," she finally told her husband. "Death, to me, would be preferable." She decided they would move to Yakima, where, she told him, "I shall make money, and you aught, with your education, to be able to get into some kind of paying business."

Bethenia opened another medical office, calling her duties "play" compared to farm life. She became active in the Woman's Christian Temperance Union, writing articles and giving addresses. Meanwhile, her would-be mogul husband piled up household debts that, in 2008 value, topped $600,000. Today, a personal debt load that large is questionable for all but the wealthy; over a century ago, it was scandalous.

Addressing a "mothers' meeting" at which she urged women to educate their daughters for employment, she told her audience, "I do not know a more pitiful object than a grown man or woman with nothing to do, and plenty of time to do it in." She could have been talking about her own husband. It was now obvious that the pioneer doctor had married unwisely once again. This time, she had no one to blame but herself.

The erudite and charming colonel loved to entertain and loved Bethenia to be the hostess, expecting her to do all the work required in addition to efforts on behalf of her medical practice, suffrage and temperance. Again, it was too much. "You are in no business here," she scolded John and ordered him back to the farm. "If you cannot get into business down there," she told him, "you can certainly see the place is kept up."

Mattie, in turn, was almost as stern with her foster mother. There was no point, she said, in "toiling all your life, making thousands and thousands of dollars . . . slaving to pay off miserable debts." Moreover, she told Bethenia, it was time she retired.

Bethenia formulated a plan: once she had saved a certain sum, she would give up her practice. By October 1905, she had reached her financial objectives and closed her North Yakima office. She didn't stay long at the farm. Two months with the colonel was enough. She left to visit friends in San Diego. Less than a year later, with a net worth far less than she had anticipated, she filed divorce papers on her ne'er-do-well husband.

But Bethenia Owens-Adair had no time for a restful, serene retirement. One fateful day, over 20 years before, Bethenia had toured Oregon's state insane asylum. There, the seed of another cause had been planted. In 1907, that seed began to flower. Well into the 20th century, mental institutions remained austere, primitive places, even when run by compassionate personnel. On her tour, however, Dr. Owens-Adair had found nothing disagreeable about the state facility or its staff. Instead, it was the patients themselves and their effect on future generations that troubled her.

"I would see to it that not one of this class should ever be permitted to curse the world with their offspring," Bethenia had candidly told the doctor in charge.

The doctor was taken aback. He knew she meant eugenics—enforced sterilization.

"Would you advocate that method?" he asked.

She would, she told him, if she wasn't a doctor. Bethenia was worried that if her private convictions were made public, she would be ostracized. She may have had less to worry about than she thought. Just a few years later, her beliefs were shared by millions of others; proponents of compulsory sterilization laws were gaining support all over the US.

Bethenia was convinced that insanity was a hereditary affliction. If the insane couldn't have children, she reasoned, the illness would likely disappear. Moreover, "loathsome victims" of "diseased reproductive organs" might be cured through castration or salpingectomy. Every patient in every mental institution, she fervently believed, should have a "simple surgical operation" to render them unable to reproduce.

This was to be Bethenia Owens-Adair's final crusade and her legacy: she would lead the way to a healthier, happier, more productive society. Bethenia drafted and introduced an Oregon eugenics law, duly passed in 1909; however, the governor then vetoed the measure. Bethenia pressed on, writing letters, articles and a book and giving speeches.

The Anti-Sterilization League mounted a fierce opposition, arguing that Bethenia and her supporters had not proven that sterilization was either effective or necessary. Eight years later, the league forced a referendum and the measure was defeated.

Finally, after a decade of effort, Bethenia's sterilization law was passed in 1917, but even then there were setbacks. The law was deemed unconstitutional. Bethenia tried again, targeting sexual offenders (which, at the time, included homosexuals), epileptics and those branded by some ill-defined standard as "moral degenerates." A new Oregon eugenics law was finally passed in 1923, and Bethenia and her supporters celebrated victory. By then, over 30 other states had similar laws.

By 1983, when the law was finally repealed, its victims numbered over 2,600 Oregon citizens. In a 2002 public ceremony, Governor John Kitzhaber told victims and rights groups, "The time has come to apologize for misdeeds that resulted from widespread misconceptions, from ignorance and from bigotry."

In the end, Bethenia's legacy was one of tragedy. Two-thirds of the victims of her eugenics law were women. Through her zealous actions, this champion of gender equality actually helped sabotage the rights of hundreds of Oregon women who were often misdiagnosed or driven mad, not by their genes, but by a myriad of external causes that often included physical or psychological abuse suffered at the hands of men.

4

Rebel Writer: Irene Baird

THEY WERE ON THEIR WAY, 100 of them! That evening, their comrades had given them a rousing send-off. The men waved down to their buddies on the wharf as the lines were slipped and the steamer to Vancouver Island backed out into Coal Harbour. A few minutes later, the black-hulled "Princess" night boat was churning the waters underneath Vancouver's almost-completed Lions Gate Bridge, headed for its home port of Victoria, BC's pretty little capital.

But it wasn't pretty where these men were going to flop the next morning. They had no rooms reserved at the elegant Empress Hotel. They wouldn't be taking afternoon tea in the hotel's spacious lobby. There was going to be none of that for these dangerous-looking Depression-era protesters.

A few hours before, they'd been rioting, ducking the tear-gas canisters arcing above Vancouver's downtown streets and the billy clubs and rubber hoses coming down on their heads. Of course, not everyone aboard this particular sailing was one of those bums getting ready for a bloody showdown at the harbourside Legislative Buildings.

Other passengers were tourists, honeymooners, businessmen—and one nicely turned out, thirtysomething woman, slight, slender and bright-eyed. By the rings on her finger, she was somebody's wife and homemaker, maybe a mother of schoolchildren. But hubby and kids weren't with her tonight. She wasn't making relaxed small talk with other women in the dining room or sitting curled up in her cosy cabin with a book.

Instead, there she was in the middle of *them*—those uncouth, unshaven louts who were slouched everywhere. The whole mob—those who weren't still pacing the darkened decks—had taken over the lounge and the card room, too. And there she sat, asking them questions, listening to them whine their crackpot philosophies and watching them, always watching. There was a hot-eyed edginess about her— it made a decent person want to turn away.

Even inside this knot of untidy, unkempt men, few knew that the woman's name was Irene "Bonnie" Baird, or that she was, in fact, hard at work. Bonnie was a novelist, and she was witnessing—she just knew it—the greatest drama of her sedate, predictable life. She would soon fashion that drama into a novel that would surprise and shock the critics of the day, a dramatic story one columnist called "one of the best books that has come out of Canada in our time."

Bonnie's own story began in England, but her upper-class family had emigrated to Vancouver Island when she was a teenager. A few years later, she was a married woman and the mother of two. Life was fine; husband Robert, an engineer, was doing well, and the kids were happy.

By the mid-1930s, Bonnie, a former schoolteacher, had discovered a creative outlet. In 1937, the name Irene Baird was on the cover of *John*, a philosophical novel about an Englishman who forsakes a successful family business for "the colonies," spurning big-city hustle for rural West Coast tranquility. Almost without a plot, certainly without hard-edged 21st-century action, the story reflects its somnolent setting. The novel's most dramatic scene occurs when John brandishes a shotgun at a neighbour who has maliciously shot and killed John's horse. Despite John's vengeful stance, his gun is unloaded, the perpetrator is never brought to justice and the beloved horse never replaced. Yet, the book found readers in North America, England, Australia and Sweden, an amazing achievement for a first-time 1930s novelist.

By the time publisher's royalties were coming in, they were likely very welcome. Robert had become one of Canada's unemployed millions. Still, the Bairds enjoyed a comfortable, easygoing life in Victoria's sedate Oak Bay municipality. That was a lot more than many others could say, and Bonnie and Robert knew it. "It was an exciting, deeply troubling time," Bonnie remembered 40 years later. Despite her enviable circumstances, she said, "This was the Depression. We were all 'have-nots' together."

By 1935, a bitter stew of anger and resentment was simmering inside idled young men. In June, 1,400 unemployed transients "rode the rods" east across the prairies on their way to Ottawa, clinging to boxcars, determined to force the federal government to provide assistance. The "trekkers" got as far as Regina, Saskatchewan. When the RCMP attempted to arrest the trek's leaders, the men's bottled-up rage and frustration bubbled over. In the melee that followed, dozens were battered and bruised and a police officer and a trekker died from their injuries. Just as unemployment figures skyrocketed again, the federal government closed labour camps set up to provide men with a little food, money and a place to sleep. Pleading financial distress, BC did the same. So, in the sweltering summer of 1938, 6,000 unemployed men found themselves in Vancouver. And so did Bonnie Baird.

"The living of the novel, the writing of it, was an adventure. An exciting time, and I had set myself an exciting task," she recalled. "I found those jobless people irresistible, urgent, challenging. I went to the job as a writer with a tremendously important assignment; how to get it down right, how to make it live, how to make Canadians see it and feel it as I was doing. I lived with the story."

It was a story of self-worth shredded by years of

helplessness, of love and even compassion ground down by all-pervasive fear and despair. Initially, Bonnie wanted to call the novel *Sidown, Brothers, Sidown,* "but the publishers were leery (understandably, perhaps, considering the temper of the times). Sit-downs were fairly new in those days. Certainly they were new in British Columbia," she explained, "and the sight of those rough-shod, rag-tag, tightly disciplined men headed for Nowheresville shook us all." The final title was *Waste Heritage.*

In the aftermath of the violence at Vancouver's main post office, where the unemployed had sat for more than a month, the still-defiant men were planning a Victoria protest. Into this maelstrom of unrest comes Baird's fictional Saskatchewan drifter, Matt Striker, who jumps off the freight train and lands in the middle of the planning for Vancouver Island's protest. *Waste Heritage* is Matt's tale, one he shares with a simple-minded companion, Eddie, whom he rescues from a club-swinging policeman, and Hazel, a young working girl eager for love and desperate for a better life.

At first, Bonnie kept her project a secret, but soon friends and family discovered her obsessive preoccupation. "My family practically gave me up; I think they feared I should be picked up with the jobless and tossed into gaol."

While protesters milled about in Victoria, Bonnie read a column about their "accommodations." The columnist said he had seen the slums of London, Paris and New York, but he could remember nothing that compared with these hovels. Bonnie had to see this for herself, but the area was all but off-limits. She knew she wouldn't pass as a reporter.

The Baird family physician, Dr. D.M. Baillie, was also Victoria's city medical officer, responsible for making a daily inspection of the buildings where the men were living. Would the doctor allow her to go with him on his rounds the next day, Bonnie asked? She promised to "look anonymous, sound speechless, and carry a small black bag—the latter to suitably describe me as a nurse!"

The good doctor was scandalized. He told Bonnie she was crazy. She confessed she was writing a book. *"Writing a book?"* the shocked physician shouted in his Scots burr. "That's the daftest thing I ever hurrd . . . of!"

Nevertheless, the next day, Dr. Baillie and "nurse" Baird made the rounds of condemned harbourfront buildings, one of which—a Gay Nineties–era brick hotel—still stands today, boarded up and abandoned. "By the time we got back into the fresh air," Bonnie recalled, "I had no more doubts about finishing *Waste Heritage* and for the next six months I hacked away as though the world were coming to an end—as in a way it was." She began recording her perceptions, including all the gritty details, and strove to articulate the emotions churning inside Matt, Eddie, Hazel and all her other characters caught up in the tumult. She accurately portrayed the men's pent-up rage: "Red-eyed, slack-shouldered, they muttered among themselves, mouths tightened by a grim, brooding anger. The feeling of anger was everywhere, raw and seething. From time to time a man sitting off by himself kept getting up and going away and vomiting."

Bonnie's protagonist, Matt Striker, expressed the crushing hopelessness of the times: "I have floated around the nine provinces so long now I don't belong in any of them . . . I don't belong in the country unless they have a war and want to shove a gun in my hand. Well Hazel maybe if that's all they have to offer I won't wait for a war. I'm not dead but I aught to be. They got no place to put me alive."

Despite her sympathy for the men, Bonnie strove to tell the complete story. "I would have lied," Bonnie explained, "if I had tried to show that radicals—that communists—were not a strong part of that organization." The more legitimate organizers of the unemployed had objectives that were just as clear as those of the much-loathed "Reds," who were manipulating these radicals to serve their own political end—the ascendancy of the Communist Party. Bonnie Baird made these objectives clear in *Waste Heritage* through this fictitious discussion of the sit-down strategy:

> Hep spoke carefully . . . "look," he said, "when a guy squats down on his tail an' stays there, he's actin' quiet and peaceful, he doesn't commit any act of violence or sabotage an' in most cases he maintains his own discipline, the same way we done here. Up until the trick gets pulled too often and the public goes fed-up on it, there's more horse-power to a sit-down than all the riots and skull-splitting

parties ever staged . . . I tell you, boy, the sit-down's got something. You got to use strategy to handle it right, dramatize it . . . by Christ, if it's handled right the sit-down can be dynamite!"

"I would have lied, too," Bonnie added, "if I hadn't shown the brutality of police forces who were afraid and who could never get as close to the men as I did . . . I would have lied if I hadn't tried to get across the reality of stores full of things to buy, and the longing of men who had no money to buy and hadn't had any for years . . . I was angry at what looked like our whole public indifference to what was happening to the Matt Strikers of Canada, and especially of British Columbia. For that reason alone I had to be dead accurate."

But *Waste Heritage* makes it clear that some members of the public were more contemptuous of unemployed protestors than indifferent. Some people were afraid of the sheer numbers of them:

Most of the places they turned him down quick and cold and the others he could tell were plain scared of him . . . that is they were scared of the eight hundred boys in town like him. One office he went into a man pulled out a one dollar bill and said he didn't want any trouble.

Matt held himself under control. "I'm not out to cause you any trouble, mister. All I want is a job, any kind of job at all. I can drive a truck or wrestle baggage or clean windows or do night watchman, pretty near any damn thing you want. Just give me the chance to prove it."

The man slipped the bill back in his pocket now he saw that Matt had not come to stick up the place. He said in a placating voice, "I haven't anything right now, maybe if you were to come around next week."

Matt knew that line by heart.

Unfortunately, despite Bonnie's scrupulous accuracy and vivid descriptions, *Waste Heritage* did not sell. "Most readable" and "Some of it sticks to the mind like burrs," enthusiastic reviewers wrote. One columnist called Bonnie's characters "the toughest yet saddest, most moving set of lads you ever heard of." Incredulous critics checked the name on the cover. How could a woman write this stuff? How'd she get that street talk? How on earth did she know what these men thought, how they felt?

Irene "Bonnie" Baird did what few writers of either gender did. In her own words, this well-dressed Oak Bay wife and mother "lived with the story" as only a rebel would and then wrote the kind of story only a rebel could write. She substituted personal passion for politics, and as one newspaper columnist marvelled, "She has, in one book, told more about the economic problems of our times than all the government reports, politicians' speeches, statistics, and blue books from Victoria to Ottawa."

Perhaps that was why the book did not sell. Even if people could find spare cash for a book, who could enjoy reading about what they're already living every day, or—Bonnie's bigger problem—what they used to live not too many months before?

Time was moving on, and by the time a Toronto publisher accepted Bonnie Baird's manuscript, it was 1939. Six months into the interminable editing and publishing process, Bonnie sat in the gallery at the legislature, watching the BC government grapple with the unemployment problem. She was desperate to see *Waste Heritage* in bookstores.

"Get it here and get it here quick," the author pleaded with her publisher. But it was already too late.

Weeks before, Germany had invaded Poland. Britain was now at war, and so was Canada. Nobody was riding the rods any more. Former transients were lined up at recruiting offices. They pulled off their worn-out pants, split shoes and grimy shirts, and pulled on new uniforms. Now everyone, including former engineer Robert Baird, had a job: defeating Hitler. Who wanted to dwell on the Depression?

If time was moving on, so was Bonnie Baird. "Is there any branch of national work in which a writer could be of service?" she asked her publisher. Indeed there was, and Bonnie found it. As the war continued, she was speaking into radio microphones and before audiences, writing pamphlets and passionately urging a unified wartime effort between the US and Canada and between men and women. In the pages of her third novel, *He Rides the Sky*, she expressed her new passion through the fictitious letters of Pete O'Halloran, a young Canadian bomber pilot in Britain, who says he is "doing the best thing with my life that was worth a damn by coming over here to join the Air Force."

After the war, Bonnie worked at Canada's famed National Film Board and later with the Department of Indian Affairs as the first woman to head a federal government information service. Through formal documents, magazine articles and poetry and fiction, she chronicled the effects of "civilization" on the Inuit people.

Waste Heritage would return. It was being taught at universities, but students couldn't find copies. Bonnie herself twice urged Macmillan, her original publisher, to reprint the book. In 1973, Macmillan agreed. Bonnie insisted the reprint had to be absolutely right. "The author is curiously tricky to deal with," complained a Macmillan executive. The edition was less than it could have been.

Irene "Bonnie" Baird died in Victoria in 1981. She would have been very pleased with the second *Waste Heritage* reprint, a handsome edition published by University of Ottawa Press in 2007, complete with a comprehensive critical introduction by the University of Toronto's Colin Hill. Through extensive research, Hill has rescued one of Canada's most underappreciated novels and its passionate author from disappearing into the past.

5

Rebels at Work: "Rosie," "Wendy" and the Shipyard Rebels

A LITTLE MORE THAN A CENTURY ago, less than 5 percent of the married women in the US were part of the labour force. Aside from a brief period during the Second World War, the percentage of employed wives and mothers didn't increase much until the 1960s.

Not all husbands were adamantly opposed to wives working outside the home. Many would have cheerfully welcomed the additional money and perhaps their wives' improved disposition. Men's reluctance was due to the fear of social stigma, which was directed more against them than their wives. "(My mother) did a little dressmaking at home, much against my father's better judgement," one anonymous Washington State woman remembered. "It was in the days when women weren't supposed to work outside the home. He felt he would be embarrassed if she worked for money. He didn't object to her working, but he didn't like people to know it."

As women's unrest grew, the stock market crashed in 1929. American first lady Eleanor Roosevelt offered some subtle job-seeker encouragement in her 1933 book, *It's Up To the Women*. "Nowadays there is a great deal of agitation as to whether married women should work or not," she began cautiously.

Three years later, a Gallup Poll revealed that 82 percent of respondents still believed wives of employed husbands should not work outside the home. It's no wonder the president's wife approached the topic with caution; the wonder is that she tackled it at all. Tens of millions of men remained unemployed as the US and Canada suffered through the long and dismal Depression. What kind of woman who enjoyed her husband's income would take a job a man could do?

However, as soup-kitchen queues lengthened and home and business foreclosures multiplied, some may have wondered when mere agitation would turn to job action. The answer came just a few years later.

* * *

To paraphrase a radio-broadcasting cliché, "We interrupt our traditional values to declare war." By 1941, millions of American and Canadian women found themselves in aircraft factories, automotive plants and shipyards. The traditional values that war interrupted were those found inside male-dominated worksites, and to a lesser extent, female-dominated homes. The reason that old values were put aside was simple: millions of men suddenly left to fight Germany and Japan.

Exactly what type of women sought shipyard employment, their motivations for doing so and how they felt about walking away at the war's end are issues clouded by wartime misconceptions and, later, sentimental reminiscences. The rebel label comes easily. These hundreds of thousands of women entered work environments once denied them. Certainly, in the minds of their parents and even many of their contemporaries, it was an accurate one.

Initially, Canada met its wartime shipyard needs through hiring the Depression's unemployed men. It had been over 20 years since a large ship had slid down the ways of a BC yard. Growth was slow, as existing shipyards had to be retooled and enlarged. At Burrard Shipyards in Vancouver, BC (destined to become the biggest shipyard in the country), the first female welder wasn't hired until the summer of 1942.

Then, things started changing rapidly. That winter, 149 women were at work in Burrard alone. The same year, 17 percent of the workers walking through Kaiser's new shipyard gates at Vancouver, Washington, were women. Women made up 11 percent of the force at Swan Lake, Oregon. One year later, 4.5 percent of BC shipyard workers were women. Although these low percentages don't seem very impressive, they reveal a significant change. Until 1941 there wasn't a single female shipyard worker in BC or the Pacific Northwest. Shipyards had been—and still were—a man's world.

So, why would a woman want to work there? "I went in the shipyards because I needed the money," wartime Burrard worker Jonnie Rankin said bluntly. She and her husband were separating, and she had three children. Others were widows or divorcees, or had absentee military husbands. Money was the motivator that propelled women into fast-track training programs. And shipyard money was the best money ever.

"It was an unbelievable amount of money, just unbelievable," recalled Betty Cleator. It was enough for Betty to quit a "well-paid" office job for shifts in a gritty, grimy Oregon shipyard. Thousands of women quit jobs in restaurants, hotels and retail stores. Before the attack on Pearl Harbor, 67 percent of Puget Sound's women employees worked in trade and service sectors. By 1945, that number had fallen to about 48 percent.

Women's wages were notoriously low, as little as $20 a month. Office work paid $60 a month. By 1943, women inside Victoria's Yarrows Shipyard were earning an average of $169 a month, 28 percent more than the wage of the average Canadian. Unions advocated equal pay for men and women, and even if that didn't always occur (Yarrows' women were earning 77 percent of men's wages in 1944), most women didn't complain. They'd never had it so good.

Most former shipyard workers interviewed in 1981 for the Oregon Historical Society's unique Northwest Women's History Project scoffed at the notion that they worked to do their bit to beat Hitler. "There's no use saying I did it for patriotism," Kathryn Blair of Portland admitted. "It was pure economics."

That's not what the American government's work and war agency representatives thought, nor business operators and their ad agency consultants, nor magazine editors, nor Hollywood producers. Surely women would do "men's work" out of a sense of duty. Most of them had these heavy-industry women all wrong. Very soon, even their iconic invention "Rosie the Riveter" was wrong, as new mass-production techniques made her "Wendy the Welder."

The better-educated, middle-class women whom the atti-tude shapers sought to entice into factories and shipyards said, "No thanks." The women who gladly pulled on heavy gloves and goggles were usually slightly older workplace veterans. Almost 30 percent of female wartime industry workers in 1942 had been in the labour force for a decade or more. Relatively affluent middle- and upper-class women followed the tradi-tion that a wife and mother had no business in the work world toiling for Uncle Sam or anybody else. If work they must, it most certainly would not be in grimy blue-collar industries, no matter what movies, ads and magazine stories told them.

In MGM's three-hour, Oscar-nominated home-front epic *Since You Went Away,* Anne Hilton (Claudette Colbert) is a shipyard worker and landlady to a household full of stock movie characters. She simultaneously shepherds her daughters (Jennifer Jones and Shirley Temple) through their youth while doing her bit for Uncle Sam. Unlike real-life shift workers, Anne certainly wasn't doing it for the money. Some of today's perceptive movie fans scoff at the notion. "I mean really, can you imagine Claudette Colbert working as a riveter in a shipyard?" asks one 2008 Amazon DVD reviewer. Moviegoers in 1943 probably couldn't imagine it either. Anne Hilton's grammar, poise and comfortable home represented the upper middle class. Dirt-under-the-fingernails work was more likely the domain of Hilton's "coloured" maid (*Gone with the Wind*'s Oscar-winning Hattie McDaniel). Still, real-life shipyard workers likely sobbed through the four-hanky box-office hit instead of laughing at it, just as MGM wanted them to.

Confusion about who sought industry work and why resulted in tens of millions of wasted dollars in job recruitment and marketing. The misconceptions had even more serious social consequences by the war's end.

Two types of media got it mostly right. One was "confession" magazines. It is hard to overestimate the power of the so-called pulps (the name referred to their low-grade paper). The leading pulp magazine, *True Story,* boasted two million subscribers. Considered trash by more affluent readers, the confession genre was unashamedly geared to the working class. The well-founded suspicion was that "true" confessions were produced by professional writers. While extolling the three Ms (monogamy, marriage and motherhood), confessions ironically dealt with incest, rape, adultery and other unseemly topics more often and openly than did sophisticated magazines.

At a time when 25-cent paperbacks were new and hardcover books luxury items, these magazines offered war-plant women, half of whom had not finished high school, easily accessible fiction. A typical *True Story* issue contained 10 short stories. Editors worked closely with the government's Office of War Information, which offered writers ideas for home-front themes and plots. The fictional road map for finding a husband led readers straight into war plants, factories and shipyards. The desired man was usually the foreman, factory owner or his son. In the story "We Shall Build Good Ships," a girl and a boy "Want Each Other, But in a Shipyard They Find There's More to Love Than the Taking."

In a case of life imitating art, women initiated BC's first and last female shipyard strike at Burrard in 1944. Women protested the firing of a woman who wore "tight clothing." While most women frowned on their colleague's "brazen performance," one female worker told the *Vancouver Sun* that the issue "is striking at the very foundation of woman's unalienable rights." And what rights were those? "No matter what the conditions and circumstances," she went on, "a woman must retain her pre-eminent right above all things to catch her man." The worker was reinstated.

In another *True Story* tale, one newcomer despises "the yards," but then "I opened my purse and took out my badge . . . It wasn't a badge of servitude after all! It was a mark of distinction, of privilege!"

Many real-life welders and ship fitters shared those sentiments. "Dirty work" meant more than big money or potential matrimony. "I had an object in mind," explained Etta Harvey. "I had a son to raise and I also wanted to prove that women were reliable and capable. I mean, it was something I had to prove to myself."

"When you chip that slag off and see that gorgeous weld underneath," remembered former Oregon waitress LueRayne Culbertson, "it was a real, real satisfying job."

The focus of home-based entertainment was the floor-model radio, the equivalent of today's satellite-fed flat-screen TV. By 1941, millions followed the trials and triumphs of over 50 daytime soap-opera heroines. The broadcast networks—the second media segment that got it right—knew their audience well, so soap operas virtually ignored war-work themes. Listeners who tuned in the shows and the sponsors' commercials were middle-class women who were washing, ironing and planning the family dinner. Consequently, not many strong-but-suffering middle-class radio heroines worked in shipbuilding or any other wartime industry. Radio's fictitious career of choice was marriage—

"Smile, girls!" And they did, because these wartime Victoria Machinery Depot employees were earning more money than they had ever earned before. ROYAL BC MUSEUM, BC ARCHIVES F-09694

getting it, keeping it, saving it—something writers and advertisers believed was also true of their listeners.

The flood of women into the shipyards forced heavy industry to change the way work was conducted. Employees usually conform to worksites. This time, employers tried to conform to their employees in order to compensate for women's limited work experience and physical strength. Jobs were redefined; ironically, this sometimes hindered women's opportunities. A 1943 survey of 131 US plants revealed that more than half had no plans to advance females, the very employees General Motors' president called "more enthusiastic and showing much better spirit" than men. Worst of all, women were denied interesting and higher-paid positions. Thousands were welders and cleaners, doing "women's work," but few were crane or drill operators. Some knew acting shy and retiring wasn't going to get them those jobs. They let their bosses know what they wanted.

"I just thought it would be interesting to operate one of those big drills," Alice Erickson, a low-level tack welder, remembered. She asked if she could try out for the job.

The drilling supervisor was caught off guard, saying, "I've never had a woman driller on my crew."

"Well, I think I can handle it," Alice said. She tried out and was hired, the first of her kind at Swan Island Shipyard in Portland, Oregon.

Others were allowed to do interesting work, but for a fraction of a man's pay. Reva Baker became a weld inspector. Her supervisor was impressed. "He said he was gonna try to get me the title because it would be like a lead man's title; it was a higher-paying job than a welding job. Well, he chickened out."

Workplace rebels often had little luck changing sexist attitudes. "The average of them was pretty nice," said Nona Pool, "but there was a lot of hardheads . . . and they thought that women were supposed to be pregnant and barefoot and 'yes, sir.'"

So, if women were doing "men's work" and making big bucks, who was minding the kids? In Oregon, it was Henry and Edgar Kaiser, the father-son industrialist team who built two major child-care centres along with their shipyards. Today, the reaction to this would be overwhelmingly positive, but in the 1940s, the innovative idea polarized communities. What the Kaisers saw as a solution to a production problem, some community daycare committees regarded as a threat to child rearing. The centres might make it too convenient for mothers to abandon their kids, especially mothers of very young children, who many felt had no business working. Initially, some mothers weren't thrilled either, believing that nobody could bring up Betsy or Bobby like they could. Some worried about whom their youngsters would be playing with—and what colour they were.

To Henry Kaiser, the centres were an integral part of "the factory of the future," embracing "shopping centres, food dispensers, banking facilities," and a host of other services. The Kaisers hired the best child-care professionals and nutritionist in the country. Funded by an employee-employer partnership, the centres were ahead of their time, providing preschool education and socialization in classrooms, exercise on playgrounds, medical assistance in infirmaries and even family take-home meals at the end of Mom's shift.

"I have never seen anything so remarkable," enthused a Woman's Bureau spokesperson. "They are open 24 hours a day and are so advanced they actually beggar description." By 1944, over 600 children were being cared for in the Kaiser centres.

North of the border, child care remained a critical issue. British Columbia mothers needy or greedy enough to work in shipyards (patriotism being the same modest motivator it was in the US) were on their own. Unlike Portland, Oregon, or Vancouver, Washington, where even the Kaisers agreed that existing child care was more than adequate, there was little daycare available in BC. "Child care was a big problem and it was talked about all the time because women worry all the time," Jonnie Rankin remembered. "Sometimes we had relatives and sometimes the kids would just be left, you know, indiscriminately around," she remembered.

Across the border, American women had clout. Forty thousand Pacific Northwest women were working inside shipyards, where they made up 27 percent of the workforce at Kaiser's three yards alone. As late as 1944, only 6 percent of BC's shipyard workers were female. Despite individual need, low numbers doomed wartime daycare initiatives. Throughout the war, there was just one recognized daycare in all of Vancouver, Strathcona Day Nursery.

Jonnie and others attempted to organize more. "We tried to. We worked at it, yeah, we worked at it. We had many committees, coming and going and petitioning and sending letters and delegations to the city hall and to Victoria to get funded for a daycare," she remembered. Sadly, organizers "didn't get it until after the war," when the desperate need had already disappeared.

Jonnie was fortunate to know Mrs. Stewart, a maid

earning $50 a month, far more than a shipyard welder, in the upper-class Shaughnessy district. "Jonnie, if you can get a job in the yards, I'll come and live with you for $25 dollars a month," Mrs. Stewart told her. Jonnie got the job, and Mrs. Stewart became "like part of the family." Others weren't so lucky. "Women had to quit even though they badly needed the money. But they just couldn't leave their children."

Then, near the end of the war, while Jonnie worked as a passer girl catching red-hot rivets, Mrs. Stewart left. Jonnie's luck held; she found a replacement. "She wasn't as good a housekeeper, but she was sweet with the kids. And I didn't care anyways; I was big and strong and could handle it all . . . I could do it [the housework] at night, and do the shopping. As long as she was good with the kids, I didn't care about anything else."

Soon, shipyard mothers had a bigger worry than nagging daycare concerns. Prices rose 29 percent between 1939 and 1945, and these women were about to lose the best-paying jobs most would ever have.

Hire women at the end of the war? Henry Kaiser seemed surprised by the reporter's question. Of course, and he knew which women, too. "The ones who consider welding a better postwar achievement than wielding a typewriter or a broom," he shot back. Henry had a question of his own for the New York Times reporter: "Do you think women are not going to demand the right to stay in industry?" he asked.

By May 5, 1945, Victory in Europe (VE) Day, pipe-shop

worker Edna Hopkins had no illusions. The boss told Edna to stop work; everyone else was celebrating.

"Well, I want to finish this pipe," she told him. "This is the last pipe I'll ever weld."

"You're kidding, Shorty," he laughed. "You'll be here tomorrow."

"You wanna bet?" The wager was on. Edna won. "That was the last pipe I ever welded. They laid me off the next day . . . The women in the pipe shop were all laid off."

Nobody on either side of the US–Canada border was too surprised by layoffs and the inevitable shipyard closings. The government, the media and popular sentiment had prepared them for the end. The men were coming back, and, "Yes!" shouted a Mobil Oil ad. "Your job is waiting for you, Soldier!" A few weeks after Japan surrendered, a Sunkist ad featuring the image of a toddler exclaimed, "Little Ones are Mighty Sweet Now!"

But wartime workers had a surprise of their own for *Ladies Home Journal*. Editors were shocked by the results of their working-women's survey. Half of those surveyed said they didn't plan to stop working after the war. A stunning 79 percent admitted they liked working better than being at home. "Jobs are more enjoyable," the magazine chided, "but homes are more important." Ironically, peacetime meant that these women would start making their own sacrifices.

Over the next year, thousands of women searched in vain to find work at former shipyard wages. Then, desperate for money, some took anything—clerking, waitressing, cleaning—at a fraction of their former pay. Most gave up, found a wage-earning man or were reunited with the one they had, and left the labour force.

Operating a crane was the highlight of Joanne Hudlicky's life: "I put everything into it I could 'cause I really wanted to do it." Like most wives and mothers after the war, Joanne Hudlicky never worked outside her home again.

Through a combination of luck, persistence and personal circumstances, a handful of the tens of thousands of female wartime heavy-industry workers managed to stay in or re-enter industry. During the happy-homemaker era of the conformist 1950s and 1960s—which social analyst Betty Friedan described as the "strange sleep"—a few shipyard rebels were doing what they wanted to do. Most had waited years for the opportunity.

"We just don't have the facilities for women," a Freightliner representative told Nona Pool in the mid-1950s when she was looking for a welding job.

"I'll bring my own potty, just bring me a curtain," she joked. She was finally hired.

In the 1970s, telephone operator Reva Baker applied for an equipment-servicing position. "It's dirty work; you have to climb ladders," her boss told her.

"I've done dirty work all my life . . . I've been up and down ladders before," she said.

Rebel Reva got the job.

6

Rebel Scientist:
Dixy Lee Ray

SHE ALWAYS GOT SO INFERNALLY HOT, standing underneath the huge studio lights. Never mind; a little discomfort was a small price to pay for the opportunity to educate and, yes, entertain folks all over the Seattle area. The middle-aged woman with the cherubic face, her dancing eyes and prominent eyebrows framed by hair bobbed in a short, mannish cut, took a deep breath and watched the film introduction flicker on the large monitor not far from the boxy grey camera.

Three, two, one! She saw the floor director's pointed finger and flashed a broad grin into the camera lens. "Hello, everyone! Welcome to *Animals of the Seashore*. I'm Dr. Dixy Lee Ray."

Academics blanched. Dr. Ray was peddling hard science—marine zoology, to be precise—as entertainment. In the mid-1950s, science was arcane and complicated; it wasn't supposed to be entertainment. But what could you expect from TV, even if it was Washington State's educational channel?

The program decision-makers at TV station KCTS had heard all about how Professor Ray delivered her lectures, and they were intrigued. Students, it seemed, either loved Ray passionately or loathed her venomously, the latter reaction being entirely understandable if you happened to be one of the snoozing University of Washington freshmen bonked with her flying chalk or blackboard eraser. And the faculty scuttlebutt! "An intemperate, feeble-minded old bitch!" one fellow professor snorted, hardly a ringing endorsement from the anointed ones who dwelled in academe's hallowed halls. Judging that the lady must be doing something right, KCTS asked her if she would consider doing it in front of their cameras. That was convenient, at least; the studios were right on the university campus.

Dixy (who hated her given name, Margaret, preferring the one evolved from her childhood nickname, "the little Dickens") thought she might give it a try. The associate professor of zoology was now "Miss Television," university detractors scoffed.

"If a scientist cannot relate what he is doing or what he believes to the layman in simple, understandable language,"

Dixy scoffed back, "then I must seriously suspect he doesn't really know what he is doing himself."

Years after she had left the studio, fascinated dads, moms and kids all over the US were watching *Animals of the Seashore* reruns. Who knew science could be so much fun? Among those viewing closer to home were the folks on the board of the Pacific Science Center. Although it had been a big hit during the Seattle World's Fair in 1962, a year later the Pacific Science Center was close to broke. Nobody wanted to stop by and learn any more. Could Miss Television help?

Dixy said yes and became the Pacific Science Center's brand-new director. Soon, all sorts of other things were new. "I'll be damned if I'm going to become a landlady to a hoary old museum," Dixy huffed. She tossed out exhibits scientists loved but nobody else gave a hoot about. Pitching for bucks and using contributions from her own modest salary, Dixy financed captivating replacements she designed herself. She begged and borrowed items everywhere, including from NASA. Invitations went out to teachers, and Dixy watched the yellow school buses arrive. The word spread: the Pacific Science Center was actually fun!

Ten years later, Dixy Lee Ray received another offer, this one from the White House. The Atomic Energy Commission (AEC) needed a new board member. The new commissioner had to be a scientist and, as directed by President Nixon, a woman.

"What would I do every day?" Dixy asked the pipe-puffing chairman, James Schlesinger.

"Anything you want to," he said, wreathed in smoke.

It seemed too good to be true. Dixy told Schlesinger her primary interest would be communications, in order to increase public understanding and promote better science education. He seemed happy with that. Dixy was certainly happy with the annual salary of $40,000, twice her Pacific Science Center pay. She agreed to move east to attend the commission's weekly meetings at its Maryland offices. Down-to-earth Dixy did it the practical way, driving there in a customized motorhome. "Why pay a fortune in rent?" asked the common-sense woman who preferred knee socks and oxfords to pantyhose and heels. "Besides, the dogs [poodle Jacques and Scottish deerhound Ghillie] like the arrangements."

Schlesinger was right. What Dixy actually did wasn't as important as what she was: female, a scientist and environment-friendly. However, if she was an environmentalist, it was on her own terms. "God save us from those who would save us!" she said more than once, referring to rabid "pseudo-environmentalists" who wanted to protect the world by sending 20th-century civilization back to the Bronze Age. Dixy was talking about consumer advocate Ralph Nader. She understood another reason why she was chosen as commissioner: the AEC saw her as its weapon against Nader.

In 1966, former lawyer Ralph Nader launched a notorious "underdog" auto-safety crusade with the exposé *Unsafe at Any Speed*. The bestselling book chronicled potentially fatal design flaws in the object of North America's desire: the four-wheeled "psycho-sexual dreamboats" (Nader's phrase) parked in every driveway. He and teams of bright young Washington law students, dubbed "Nader's Raiders," were soon attacking sanitation levels in meatpacking plants, coal-mine and pulp-mill pollution, and the government's own corrupt Federal Trade Commission. Nader's future target was the very industry Dixy Lee Ray was now a part of: nuclear energy.

The AEC had 90,000 employees responsible for both developing nuclear sites and ensuring their safe operation. Dixie knew that much, but little else. On the way to Maryland, she steered her 28-foot motorhome through the entrances of government-owned nuclear facilities, enrolling in her own crash courses in nuclear physics and atomic energy. She had never been so excited. There were so many brilliant minds and so much potential. "What is it we could not do?" she asked, contemplating a new "wonder" age of nuclear advancement. Plant personnel were excited, too. Most of them had never even seen an AEC commissioner before, and they embraced Dixy as one of their own.

Not everyone shared Commissioner Ray's rosy, science-ensures-our-future scenario. Many felt that scientific applications, such as disease prevention through food irradiation, a process Dixy advocated, imperilled mankind's future.

"Nuclear fission power is unsafe, unnecessary and unreliable," Nader later told TV viewers watching the nuclear power debate. As he did with car safety, clean air and other Raider causes, Nader used the media to advance anti-nuke sentiment and ensure sustained public outrage, not to educate, as Dixy once had. Dixy was outraged, too, and was to remain that way for the rest of her life, but her outrage was directed toward Nader and others who she believed substituted rhetoric for sound scientific evidence. Critics of irradiated food, for example, "fail to provide facts to support their position," she said.

Sadly, Dixy and Ralph never went toe-to-toe publicly, despite political and business interest in exposing Nader's scientific ignorance. Dixy had watched Nader interrupt and browbeat opponents while forging an emotional bond with his audience. She had only one demand for a potential TV appearance with him: the adherence to formal rules of debate. A date was set. According to Dixy's media advisor, Lou Guzzo, when Nader learned of Dixy's demand, he "suddenly developed another conflicting engagement on his calendar," and the TV debate never occurred.

"No industry is more closely regulated than the nuclear industry," Dixy told people attending community workshops she had designed for those "not sure about this nuclear stuff." She also commented, "In twenty years, only seven people lost their lives in atomic accidents, while 850,000 died in automobile accidents; 300 people choke to death every year while eating."

In the end, it didn't matter. Nader's campaign achieved its objective, often indirectly, by ensuring that delays and additional regulations made future plants uneconomical. In the 1970s, nuclear-generating capacity grew more than 700 percent (an oil crisis had President Nixon calling for a 1,000 additional reactors by 2000). In the 1980s, it was down to 140 percent. By 1999, the increase in capacity had plummeted to less than 5 percent.

According to Dixy, an "emotional charlatan playing on people's fear" (Nader) and "flicker idols" (Jane Fonda and Robert Redford) were helping America become "a third-rate power in the world."

"What do any of them know about nuclear physics?" Dixy asked. But they didn't need to know about physics. All they needed to know was what Dixy knew: how to make headlines.

In 1973, Dixy made headlines again by becoming AEC chairman. Under Dixy's direction, the exhaustive, forward-looking report *The Nation's Energy Future*, which included a prescient public-private Pioneer Synthetic Fuels Program and a host of other recommendations, was completed and submitted to President Nixon in December 1973. It was a fitting going-away present.

The AEC had been beset by external attacks and internal

problems. When Dixy realized the AEC's reactor division had never submitted a budget, she turned financial attack dog and sicced a review audit on the division. The result was an extensive reorganization. A little over a year later, the AEC split into the Nuclear Regulatory Commission and the Energy Research and Development Administration. By this time, Dixy had accepted an offer from Secretary of State Henry Kissinger to become Assistant Secretary of State for Oceans and International Environment and Scientific Affairs (OES).

Dixy lasted there just five months. She felt little joy in dealing with bureaucrats. She had difficulty understanding what the State Department's policies, and those of her own bureau, were supposed to be. "Just read Dr. Kissinger's speeches," suggested his equally confused deputy secretary.

It was hard to ask the "egocentric and arrogant" Secretary of State himself. Often out of the country, Kissinger rarely made an appearance in the State Department's offices. But Dixy was also frustrated by something far more important: "Mostly it was because of the position decisions he would take in the fields of science and technology [in] which I felt I had more expertise than he. But he never consulted the assistant secretaries. He made all the decisions himself."

Dixy received no plaudits or applause for the quick action that ensured nuclear material and assets did not fall into the hands of the North Vietnamese army. Detractors said it was a wasted effort, since the communists didn't know how to use the plant.

The final straw came when the State Department declared that the US would not sell nuclear information, equipment and materials to Brazil, which needed assistance in providing electrical energy to its people. According to Dixy, "Kissinger and Co." had caved in to anti-nuke agitators. Brazil simply bought everything from Germany, and the US lost over one billion dollars in sales. Privately, Dixy accused her own department's executive of behaving "like a bunch of goddam fools," but she also shared her feelings with the *New York Times*. Kissinger's assistant phoned to tell her that the boss was not amused.

Dixy decided she no longer cared how Kissinger felt. She strode into his office to tell him she was resigning. "You'll have to prepare a briefing paper outlining the purpose of the conference you request and giving details of the subject," Kissinger's secretary blithely informed her. Dixy stalked off and wrote him a letter instead.

After writing to Kissinger, Dixy wrote President Gerald Ford a warning letter stating that the US had "too great a reliance on imported energy whose price and security of supply we are powerless to influence." She likely was referring to decisions about domestically developed alternative fuels or a ramp-up of nuclear energy. "Painful decisions are needed," she added, acknowledging that the available alternatives might not be universally accepted. Nevertheless, Dixy maintained, "Our need for reliance on solid fuels—coal and uranium—is real and must be recognized." It would be over 30 years before uranium-fuelled nuclear energy would be "recognized" as a potentially necessary source of domestic energy.

Dixy was already thinking of the next phase of her professional life. "What would you say if I told you I am thinking seriously of returning to Washington [State] to run for governor?" she asked Lou Guzzo.

If they were a little vague about what Dixy had been doing in Washington, DC, the folks in Washington State remembered her TV and Pacific Science Center days. On the campaign trail, Guzzo recalled, "The combination teacher-and-homespun-neighbor approach bowled them over. None of it was improvised or contrived," he insists. "I couldn't have written the script for Dixy's campaign tactics if I had tried." Guzzo uncovered a weakness of Dixy's most serious opponent, John Spellman. The self-assured media favourite tended to lose his cool under direct criticism. In a series of four TV debates, Dixy let fly with pointed comments and incisive questions. The rules had suddenly changed, and her male opponent no longer knew how to play the game. "I don't think anyone knew how to run that campaign," Spellman later complained. "We [Spellman's team] had a lot of debate . . . could you attack, do you give offense?" Sympathetic male reporters sided with Spellman.

Dixy's victory, a 7,000-vote squeaker, was finally acclaimed at 4 a.m., November 2, 1976. Dixy kicked off her shoes, rested her weary stockinged feet on a chair in front of her and shouted, "How sweet it is!"

Sweet turned to sour minutes later. As cameras zoomed in and microphones bobbed, Dixy couldn't resist a dig at the big-city press, "Our success tonight reflects the failure of the newspapers to elect the people they wanted elected," she grinned. "They backed the wrong horse."

The big-city media in Tacoma, Seattle and Spokane never forgave that winning horse and gave her the spurs relentlessly over the next four years. Balky Dixy made it easy for them. For one thing, she was a woman. "A few reporters simply could not acknowledge that a woman could do a good job as governor," Guzzo contends.

Not necessarily so, believed another rebel, Adele Ferguson, who broke media barriers as a controversial journalist. Ferguson often defended Dixy, only to be scorned. "I didn't even know she was ticked at me," Ferguson recalled, "though I probably have given her reason. I thought I wrote as much favorable stuff about her as bad. Maybe she only reads the bad."

When stories appeared after the governor's regular news conferences, even savvy former *Seattle Post-Intelligencer* editor Guzzo found that "The nature and amount of distortions were a shock."

"About 90 percent of what went on in the press conference was not reported. And what was reported was not accurate," Dixy told Tacoma's Channel 13 after viewing the conference tapes herself.

In the spring of 1977, Governor Ray decided to ban the conferences. Although she granted interviews to most reporters on an individual basis, her press-conference decision further alienated the media. RAY TRIES POLICY BEHIND CLOSED DOORS, shrieked the *Post-Intelligencer.* Not true, Ray contended, organizing a series of town hall meetings to speak with citizens directly. The press could attend or not; she didn't care.

One happy day at Dixy's rustic hobby-farm home on little Fox Island, a sow gave birth to 11 piglets. Dixy named each one after a reporter. A year later, she treated the media to sausage made from the pigs.

By 1977, as the environmental movement gained momentum, most astute politicians knew something that the marine biologist–governor had apparently forgotten: oil and water don't mix. Where was Alaska going to ship all the oil sitting in its port of Valdez? Dixy had the answer: Cherry Point, Washington State. "If we were to devise the best place to take this oil, this would be the place," Dixy stated confidently. "The safest way to transport oil is the most direct way, where we have to handle it least. The most efficient and economical route is into the Strait of Juan de Fuca, and I can see no element of increased risk."

Others could, however. RAY'S OIL SPILLS VIEWS MISGUIDED, two scientists told the *Post-Intelligencer.* Others argued there wasn't enough room in the strait for the massive tankers to travel safely.

"Look how much water we have on all sides," the governor pointed out from the bridge of the *ARCO Fairbanks,* as she

Washington State governor Dixy Lee Ray, ca. 1980. PORTRAITS OF STATE GOVERNORS COLLECTION, WASHINGTON STATE ARCHIVES

"steered" the 900-foot-long supertanker through Puget Sound for five minutes. The media clip only gave environmental activists more ammunition.

When the legislature prohibited supertankers, Dixy vetoed the legislation. In Washington, DC, environmentally friendly senator Warren Magnuson stepped in. The one-time Ray supporter tacked an amendment that banned Puget Sound oil ports onto a congressional bill designed to protect marine mammals. Checkmate. Magnuson not only knew how to get votes, but how to keep them, too.

In less than three years, Dixy had alienated the media, members of her own Democratic Party and a growing number of concerned citizens, including the environmentally conscious and many women, who were outraged when the governor reconsidered her pledge to re-establish the state's Women's Council. Dixy had given them a hint about her feelings in the *New York Times* just days after she was elected, however: "Stop brooding about being a woman," she had scoffed. "If you want to do something, then train yourself."

Governor Dixy Lee Ray lasted only one term, but remained in the public eye. She was good at making headlines: DIXY: CHERNOBYL ACCIDENT WAS NOT A CATASTROPHE; KEEP COOL ABOUT GLOBAL WARMING, DIXY ADVISES. With Lou Guzzo, Dixy published two "common-sense" environmental books. "We have been panicked into spending billions of dollars to cure problems without knowing whether they are real," she wrote in *Trashing the Planet*. In her second book, *Environmental Overkill*, she argued that it was "just as wrong to exaggerate the seriousness of environmental issues as it is to downplay the remarkable resilience and recovery powers of the earth."

Environmental Overkill embraced issues as diverse as global warming, food and population. Dixy named the media and the education system as unwitting co-conspirators in "spreading propaganda" for environmental crusades. First, she said, the public jumps to conclusions; then it jumps on the bandwagon. This, according to Dixy, leads to "enviro-hysteria" that results in millions of wasted taxpayer dollars spent in dubious campaigns and in defending lawsuits filed by the hysteria's real victims: the owners of ruined businesses and their laid-off employees.

At the time Dixy Lee Ray was writing *Environmental Overkill*, Vice-President Al Gore had become a self-appointed environmental champion, a role that put him squarely in the scientist's crosshairs. In Dixy's mind, a far greater danger to the American public than Gore's 1990s preoccupation, chemical waste, was "a vice-president who not only predicates his policies and actions on rumour, unsupported charges and unscientific reports, but ignores the truth because it could counter his political aspirations."

It wasn't the truth that derailed Gore's 2000 presidential bid. It was a vote-splitting independent candidate and—ironically—fellow environmental watchdog Ralph Nader. Once out of politics, Gore embraced a new *cause célèbre*, global warming. His relentless crusade earned him a share in a Nobel Prize (with the Intergovernmental Panel on Climate Change), and his documentary *An Inconvenient Truth* won an Academy Award. By then, the rebel scientist could no longer present a spirited rebuttal of Gore's advocacy, as she had in the past.

"Whatever happened to healthy skepticism?" Dixy had asked *Trashing the Planet* readers. Skepticism was alive and well, and as she discovered, some was directed at *Trashing the Planet*. Even more was directed at her final, more ambitious book. Long after she was laid to rest, *Environmental Overkill* continued to provoke strong emotional reactions from readers. Sadly, some of the most pointed criticism came from scientists and academics Dixy would have regarded as her peers. In their professional analyses, they tersely dismissed some of Dixy's statements on climate change as "nonsense." Her opinions on the ozone layer and ultraviolet rays "either ignore or misrepresent scientific evidence, and they are based upon poor scholarship."

Was Dixy ever anguished by such rebuffs? Not at all, maintains Lou Guzzo, who knew the author better than anyone outside her family. "Dixy never lost her temper" with detractors, Guzzo says, "but she held her ground."

Dixy Lee Ray died in 1994, at her home on Fox Island.

7

Rebel Politician:
Grace McCarthy

THE SECOND WORLD WAR WAS almost over, and a promising future awaited a BC Lower Mainland teenager who was destined to become a political legend. In 1944, a vivacious 17-year-old Vancouver high-school graduate cashed in a $50 war bond and started a florist shop. A shoe salesman's daughter, Grace McCarthy had business in her blood. Within a few years, cash registers were ringing in five Grayce Florists outlets. This was during an era when few women ran anything beyond a vacuum cleaner or washing machine.

Grace was behind the counter when a "customer" spotted exactly what he wanted. Not flowers, but the store's owner. He recruited Grace as a candidate for parks board commissioner, because, he told her, "You know all about flowers and plants." That made sense, but as the former chair of the Vancouver Board of Trade, Grace also knew how to get things done.

Half a century ago, women in political office were a novelty. One reason was their domestic duties. Grace was a wife and mother, too. However, she had something most 1950s women didn't have: a supportive family. Her husband, Ray, told Grace that he and their three children would back her political ambitions all the way, but it still wasn't easy.

"I see by the paper you're running for parks board," another customer remarked.

"Yes, I am. First time," Grace replied, pleased at the recognition.

"Well, that's great, Grace, and I'd vote for you if you weren't a woman."

Despite this gender discrimination, Grace won her seat on the board. A decade later, in 1966, she was elected to BC's Social Credit (Socred) government as the MLA for Vancouver-Little Mountain. As a successful business owner, it was only natural that Grace would embrace the Socreds' big-business, free-enterprise tenets, and it was her passion for commerce that would leave its mark on BC. Shortly after the election, she was appointed to the cabinet. During the boom years of the '50s and '60s, former hardware retailer W.A.C. ("Wacky") Bennett led the Socreds to victory seven times. But Grace's star was rising in Bennett's twilight. In 1972, the Socreds fell to the New Democratic Party (NDP).

The elderly Bennett resigned. His son, Bill, became Socred leader and hired party president Grace McCarthy to rebuild their party. The once-potent political force had fewer than 500 paid-up members. While Bennett tangled with the NDP in the legislature, Grace was shaking hands all over the province. During her weeks of meetings, she read out the latest door-to-door recruitment results to her audiences (likely in a bid to build good-natured rivalries between constituencies) and spent evenings instructing locals how to sign up new members. Three years later, 75,000 five-dollar memberships had been purchased. Her extraordinary success shocked even cynical media representatives.

One of the many impressed by Grace's efforts in "mounting an army of support after the defeat of W.A.C. Bennett," was the former mayor of Surrey, BC, Bill Vander Zalm. While florist Grace McCarthy had been building her chain of Vancouver flower stores, Vander Zalm was an 18-year-old Dutch immigrant trying to keep his family's flower business alive in the wake of his father's heart attack. The teenager went on the road pitching bulbs to greenhouse operators and florists like Grace McCarthy. A year later, in 1953, Bill was the owner of Art Knapp's Nurseries, conducting parking-lot plant auctions from a pickup truck. A decade later, he was behind one of his many nursery counters when worried Surrey residents told him the town council was about to turn a park into a gravel pit. "Why don't you help us fight this thing?" they pleaded.

He tried—and failed—and then realized that "the best way to beat them is to join them." The next year, Bill Vander Zalm was sitting on the Surrey council. By 1969, Bill was Surrey's controversial mayor, rooting out supposed welfare fraud and ordering young welfare recipients to work in the fields for $25 a day. Two years later, as a federal government candidate, Bill promised to come down hard on drug dealers and wife deserters, cut off welfare deadbeats and revise education. He lost, but watched for another political opportunity. That opportunity came with the party that Grace McCarthy had rebuilt. Vander Zalm became a Socred member in May 1975.

Decades later, while extolling Grace's "great organizational skills," Vander Zalm also remembered that she could be "extremely manipulative," a descriptor no doubt triggered in part by her ability to "manipulate" Vander Zalm himself. In what would become a moment of extreme irony, Grace persuaded the former Surrey mayor to run as a Socred candidate in the November 1975 provincial election.

Urging voters to "Get BC Moving Again," the Socreds swept back into power. Bill Bennett rewarded Grace well, making her deputy premier, provincial secretary and minister of tourism. Vander Zalm became minister of human resources.

A recovery budget designed to offset the NDP's $3.6-billion deficit raised government revenues by increasing

Grace McCarthy at the 1976 opening of the University of British Columbia's Museum of Anthropology. "Amazing Grace" went from running Grayce's chain of florist shops to running provincial government departments. UBC ARCHIVES 5.2/266-7

cigarette taxes and hospital day rates. In addition, the transport minister doubled BC's ferry fares, causing visits to beautiful Vancouver Island to plummet by 30 percent. Grace McCarthy, the minister of tourism, screamed in protest. Bennett hastily dumped the transport minister, and Grace redoubled her efforts with a $100,000 marketing campaign promoting BC tourism that included full-page "Island Fever" ads. Two summers later, with weeks of holidays still to come, a record-breaking 7 million tourists had visited "super, natural BC," and "General" Grace was deploying her tourist troops for the ski season.

Movies were good business, the Socreds' supersaleswoman decided. In 1978, she created the BC Film Commission, supporting domestic productions while welcoming Los Angeles filmmakers to "Hollywood North." Since then, BC-based movie productions have contributed billions of dollars to the provincial economy.

What Vancouver needed, Grace told the BC hospitality industry, was a trade and convention centre. Because the city lacked facilities, BC had lost international conventions worth $13.5 million in one year. Soon, Grace was promoting a $25-million waterfront convention centre. NDP critics carped that the costly project would only benefit big business. Grace disagreed, saying everyone would profit from the trickle-down business the conventions would attract.

As potential partners grew nervous about the escalating costs of the proposed waterfront convention facility, the premier announced the project was "postponed indefinitely." Postponed—but not cancelled.

Bill Bennett and Grace McCarthy then quietly went back to work to figure out how to slide the project off the shelf. The solution came with the World's Fair, Expo 86. By spring 1982, the federal government had announced it would build

Canada Place, a stunningly designed Expo showpiece on the vacant waterfront site that had been earmarked for the convention centre. After Expo closed four years later, Canada Place was turned over to the provincial government, and Grace McCarthy's vision was realized. Today, the Vancouver Convention Centre (enlarged for the 2010 Olympics), hosts over 300 events annually. In 2008 alone, the centre generated $213 million in economic activity.

As the 1979 election (which the Socreds subsequently won) drew near, a government researcher addressed a group of party faithful in a small room in a suburb of Victoria. He was teaching them how to fake pro-government letters to the editor. Unfortunately, one of the "students" in the room was a local newspaper reporter. The resulting exposé was dubbed "Lettergate," but soon could have been named "Tapegate." A *Vancouver Sun* newshound sniffed out a cassette on which the same hapless researcher was telling Socred constituency presidents, "We do play dirty and we don't really worry about that too much."

Deputy Premier Grace McCarthy denied any knowledge of the tape. As another MLA admitted, "Nobody listened to the damn things." But if someone—Grace, perhaps—had lent an ear, the affair might have been avoided. The man who contracted the taping and approved the content of 170 "how-to" cassettes before they were mailed was Grace's executive assistant, George Lenko, who, suspicious columnist Allen Garr noted, "does not sneeze without Grace's permission."

In the premier's absence, Grace spoke for the government, distancing it and herself from the unethical bumbling. Dirty tricks, she told Garr, were "very stupid." Did she know Lenko arranged the taping? That was a question to ask of the party, "not of me," she replied. Complaints "should *not* be laid at the foot of the government." But that's where they were laid, because not only did the party researcher resign, so did one conscience-stricken government employee, a former radio newsman who not long before had been reporting government scandals to Victoria listeners. In his duties for the deputy provincial secretary, he allegedly had written a fake letter with a phony signature.

By the time the premier returned, the fires of controversy were licking at his office door. Bennett promised that such lamentable behaviour would not happen again. Grace McCarthy—having addressed another party gathering where "dirty tricks" strategies were discussed after she had left—felt the heat. Many more fires flared up, but it was mostly other cabinet ministers who got burned, and none more often than Bill Vander Zalm.

When Vander Zalm had been sworn in as human resources minister for the new government, back in 1975, he had warned that his staff was "gonna turn up piles of fraud." The zealous welfare crackdowns had the *Vancouver Sun* calling his actions "a reign of terror." Instead of acting as minister of social welfare, the newspaper lamented, he was acting as "minister *against* social welfare."

112

Then, in the early 1980s, BC was rocked by recession. The province's unemployment rate soared to over 13 percent. Forestry, BC's sputtering economic engine, delivered just 40 percent of its previous revenue to public coffers.

In 1982, municipal affairs minister Bill Vander Zalm cut grants to municipalities. His proposed Land Use Act also reorganized the planning and zoning decision-making process so that he could make decisions with no public hearings and no appeals. Loud protests by mayors were too hot for the government to handle, and the house adjourned without passing the legislation. When a frustrated and angry Vander Zalm labelled his own colleagues "gutless," Bennett decided it was time for another cabinet shuffle and blessed every child and parent in BC with the rogue MLA as minister of education. Even in the recessionary times, Vander Zalm's belt-tightening—$60 million in school-district cuts—appeared excessive. By 1983, as both government and minister plummeted to new lows in popularity, Vander Zalm quit.

When Bill Bennett had ended Vander Zalm's troublesome tenure as human resources minister in 1978, he had given the sensitive and costly portfolio to Grace McCarthy. Soon, Madam Minister was bringing her powerful, big-business leadership qualities to social legislation by leading "the revision and complete change" to government social assistance. After 2 years of planning and another 11 months of significant government debate and public input, the new

Family and Child Service Act was proclaimed in 1981. "Our responsibility in the Ministry of Human Resources is to protect children," Grace told the legislature. That meant helping low- and fixed-income parents meet daycare costs, enforcing court-ordered child maintenance payments and fighting child abuse. To do that, Grace introduced the 24-hour Child Help Line, an innovative service later adopted by other Canadian provinces.

"Today we have a level of social services to be envied in all of the world," Grace proudly told MLAs, and she backed up the boast by tabling a new budget over 18 percent larger than the previous one.

Then, recession hit. While Vander Zalm was eliminating municipal grants and cutting education funding, Grace was making tough and unpopular human resources decisions. In spite of it all, the Socreds—and Grace—managed another election victory in 1983.

The economy improved slowly, and with Expo 86 about to give BC an unparalleled global profile, Premier Bill Bennett decided the timing was right to announce his resignation. However, for Grace, his timing could not have been worse. "I was very serious about running [for party leader] at that time," she recalled, but Expo 86 had opened just three weeks before. As provincial secretary, Grace was in charge of Expo 86 protocol. How could she possibly run for leadership and fulfill all her duties? But Grace did run, dashing to leadership meetings "at all hours of the day and night. I would leave my home in the morning, run over to Expo itself and welcome some dignitary . . . then run back to the car and drive out to Langley for some meeting." Other leadership hopefuls were unburdened by governmental priorities and distractions. Their leadership races were much easier to run. "If it wasn't a plot, it certainly could have been," Grace recalled ruefully.

Meanwhile, Socred members begged Bill Vander Zalm to become a leadership candidate. But Vander Zalm was preoccupied with the development of his $7 million Christian theme park, Fantasy Gardens, and had not forgotten the many bitter controversies and disappointments he had suffered during his time in office. He turned down all requests. Still, he must have been surprised when he received a telephone call from Grace McCarthy.

Grace realized it was critical that the party elect someone who had the experience and the obsessive drive of a true political leader. Grace thought she had it . . . but could she win? Deeply concerned that the party would choose an unqualified newcomer as its new leader, Grace made the decision to put her party first, at the potential cost of her own victory.

"Grace sort of convinced me that I should go in," Vander Zalm admitted later. "Look, you've got to run," he recalled her telling him, "I think you are a good candidate."

When the leadership convention was over, Vander Zalm was premier of the province. Promising reporters he would "bring to government high moral standards based on true Christian principles," Vander Zalm instead unravelled a string of abuses of power that had jaded journalists shaking their heads in disbelief.

To understand Grace McCarthy's position during this period, we must understand the political phenomenon known as caucus and cabinet solidarity. While they might see and hear political evil, MLAs must "speak no evil." Even cloistered in cabinet chambers, ministers who challenge colleagues or their premier do so at their political peril. Solidarity is an unspoken, unquestioned tradition.

An abrupt government reorganization meant that the premier, rather than his ministers, would now appoint deputy ministers, who, Grace recalled, "were told very clearly that they were to report directly to the premier through David Poole," the new and all-powerful deputy premier. "The new ministers were very concerned . . . they didn't know their portfolios at all and they had deputies who knew them like the back of their hand." Still, it wasn't enough to make Grace rebel against the autocratic Vander Zalm.

By late 1987, after a period of severe labour unrest, a *Vancouver Sun* poll showed 56 percent of British Columbians unhappy with Vander Zalm's performance, and things were about to get even worse for the premier.

In a landmark ruling in January 1988, the Supreme Court of Canada declared the federal abortion law discriminatory, making abortions easier to obtain. Vander Zalm, a staunch Catholic, regarded abortion as a sin and decided the provincial government medical plan wouldn't pay for it, even in cases where the fetus was severely deformed. Women with no money for the procedure would have no choice but to carry the baby to term.

The premier was besieged by reporters. "What about a 14-year-old girl who gets raped in a park and becomes pregnant?" asked one. "Are you saying you won't provide funding for her?"

"There can't be any exceptions," the premier answered.

Now the media smelled blood and closed in for the kill. The desperate premier shut his eyes and covered his ears. "Don't ask me those questions," he groaned, "I don't want to hear them." David Poole rushed to the rescue as Vander Zalm backpedalled away from the snarling news pack.

The public backlash was overwhelming. Even 55 percent of Socred members were opposed to the policy. Grace McCarthy and six other ministers broke ranks, publicly declaring their disagreement with the premier, wanting, at the very least, rape and incest exemptions. The wall of cabinet solidarity had cracked, and rebellious Grace would help to bring it tumbling down.

By 1986, the government's BC Enterprise Corporation (BCEC) held over 10,000 acres of land. As minister of economic development, Grace was responsible for BCEC. Perhaps the single most valuable property in the crown corporation's holdings was the 205-acre Expo 86 site, just a few minutes from downtown Vancouver. The government had decided to get out of the development business, and Grace instructed the BCEC to begin a bidding process to sell the Expo site.

Six months after the formal notice of sale, the premier told the media he was "upset with the [sale] process because it's taking too long . . . it's costing bundles per month." There was, he admitted, "a bit of friction between the premier's office and [Grace's BCEC] board." Over the next few months, the premier repeatedly insinuated himself into the formal bidding process, not simply because it was taking too long, but also because, as he explained later, "there was no evident opportunity for other proposals."

Nevertheless, at least one BC proposal was received. It came from Vander Zalm's long-time friend and leadership-campaign fundraiser, Peter Toigo. There wouldn't have been a problem if Toigo had abided by BCEC rules; however, the two, along with David Poole (whom the premier eventually appointed to the BCEC board itself), appeared to have made their own rules. Unbeknownst to Grace, Vander Zalm's office had allowed Toigo to inspect the BCEC books, giving him a clear advantage over all others bidding for the incredibly valuable property.

During a regular cabinet meeting, the premier suddenly presented Grace and other surprised ministers with a letter from Peter Toigo offering $445 million for all the BCEC assets, not just the Expo lands. Grace erupted. She was opposed to any negotiation with Toigo; the Expo process was already underway. Grace had some supporters, but so did the premier. Cabinet decided to change the nature of the sale.

Personally humiliated by the premier's behind-the-scenes manoeuvring, Grace was also outraged that he was subverting the sale process and told him so the next day in what veteran *Sun* reporters called "an emotional tirade." Vander Zalm said she was overreacting. She went public, telling reporters, "The premier's office should not have been involved."

Now other bidders would be invited to make another proposal for all BCEC's assets, as Toigo had done, or any of a number of other combinations of assets. Bidders wouldn't come back, the worried BCEC president warned Grace after the cabinet meeting. Having spent weeks and hundreds of thousands of dollars on an initial offer and development plans, what bidder would cheerfully go back to the drawing board to formulate a second response to the cabinet's loosey-goosey criteria?

Grace called to make an appointment with Vander Zalm but, as usual, David Poole intercepted her request and wanted to hear what she and the BCEC president had to say. Poole walked into Grace's office carrying his briefcase. Inside it, he said, was Toigo's offer. "I'd like to get a copy of that," Grace said across her coffee table.

"Well, I'll have to get authorization from the premier

before I can do that," Poole told the veteran cabinet minister. Grace was incensed and said she resented the premier's interference in the Expo lands sale.

"I take my directions from the premier. I don't take directions from you, Grace," Poole shot back. Then he let it slip that he had also phoned Toigo to tell him about the cabinet's decision on buying BCEC assets. It was insider information, pure and simple.

"Absolutely disgusting," Grace told him.

Alone again, she wrote the premier a letter. It was clear that Mr. Toigo "is not at arm's length in his relationship to our government." His access to information and influence on the process was "totally inappropriate." But the very first sentence was the bombshell: "I tender my resignation from the government."

The resignation of the minister thousands of Socred members called "Gracie" and "Amazing Grace" would have devastated the slipping party. The public repercussions were too horrid to contemplate. Grace slipped the letter into her desk drawer.

A few days later, an emotional Grace McCarthy managed to see the premier. She couldn't tolerate what was going on, she told him, and felt she had no choice but to resign. Again, the premier told her she was overreacting. Maybe, but Grace shared her concerns with Attorney General Brian Smith, BC's top cop.

Concerns were being shared inside the premier's office

as well, but they were concerns about Grace. "David Poole and (Finance Minister) Elwood Veitch, among others, had warned me of the danger in Grace's ambitions and the extent to which she might go to attain her objective," explains Vander Zalm. Grace's spirited but unsuccessful 1986 leadership bid had made that "objective" clear. But Vander Zalm recognized her as an extremely effective minister. He admired her political acumen and also understood how much party members loved "Gracie."

Grace was shocked when she learned from the premier himself that Toigo knew details of the front-running bid from Chinese billionaire Li Ka-shing. She also learned Toigo was on his way to China to meet with Li's group. To the relief of everyone but the premier and Toigo, BCEC persuaded Li's people to cancel the meeting. Vander Zalm called Grace and complained that the cancellation was appalling. Grace disagreed with her boss; he hung up on her. The next day, Grace wrote another resignation letter; however, worried that if she quit now, the inappropriate Toigo bid might be successful, she filed the letter away once again.

Toigo's final offer was now $500 million—strangely enough, the same amount as Li Ka-shing's confidential bid. By the time a member of the opposition rose in the legislature and asked, "Do you know what insider information is all about, Mr. Premier?" the *Sun* had documented at least 10 occasions when the premier or David Poole had intervened on behalf of Peter Toigo.

At the unveiling of Li Ka-shing's winning proposal, Grace beamed at the cameras, leaned into the microphone and said, "I feel great and I feel great having the premier here . . . we're together and delighted." Grace was also relieved. BCEC had selected the best bid despite all the interference, and this public show of solidarity successfully masked a stop-the-presses development. Smiling Grace McCarthy knew that the RCMP was investigating the BC premier.

In July 1988, as the premier shuffled his cabinet, Grace knew the time was right. The Expo sale was complete. Grace had demanded the premier move Poole out of government. He had refused. The week before, Attorney General Brian Smith had publicly resigned. Grace refused appointments as provincial secretary and minister of tourism, portfolios she had once held so proudly. She told the reporters crowding around her desk she was resigning. The cabinet rebel did not mince words: "Unelected officials have more power than they deserve in the premier's office and David Poole very definitely is one of those people."

Grace's attitude could not have been a surprise to the premier, who likely felt her resignation was motivated more by political aspirations than moral principles. "I believe that Grace McCarthy had a bag full of plans for taking over the leadership of the Social Credit party and becoming the premier," Vander Zalm said 20 years later.

At the Social Credit annual convention that fall, members reaffirmed Bill Vander Zalm's leadership, but over 30 percent of the delegates voted to scrap the usual secret ballot that might have led to a vote of non-confidence—and a new leader.

"A sad day for democracy," Grace lamented to a reporter.

"Why don't you knock it off, Grace," an angry party member yelled out. "Haven't you done enough damage already?"

Delegates did not choose a leader who might have instituted new, popular policies. Instead, wrote newspaper columnist Vaughn Palmer, "They ensured Vander Zalm would survive to lead them further along on the road to ruin."

It wasn't labour unrest that finally brought down Bill Vander Zalm, nor abortion controversy, education-system chaos or attempts to thwart the Expo 86 lands sale process. It was charges of abuse of power over another property, Fantasy Gardens, the theme park the premier indicated he had previously sold. But he hadn't sold all of it. Moreover, as premier, he used his influence to assist the new purchasers and then lied about it during an official investigation. On the evening of April 2, 1991, TV viewers tuned into CBC news and heard, "He broke the rules and he's gone." Unapologetic Bill Vander Zalm had been forced to resign.

"I have never seen anything quite like this before," a subdued Grace McCarthy told CBC television. It was, she said, "not a good day in our history."

With the leadership convention looming, many Socreds pleaded with Grace to run and save the ailing party, but not all party members supported her. Some blamed the rebel for the party's woes and backed interim leader Rita Johnston, a veteran cabinet minister and faithful Vander Zalm supporter. Johnston's loyalty was rewarded when she became official leader and premier—but only briefly.

NDP leader Mike Harcourt was one of those who was glad Johnston had been chosen Socred leader. He was thankful he wouldn't have to battle "Amazing Grace" in the October 1991 election. Almost all Socred candidates—including Grace—went down to defeat. The final tally was 51 seats for the NDP and just 6 for the Social Credit Party. Rita Johnston stepped down, and Grace became party leader.

"I fell into the trap of being persuaded that I was the only one who could save the party," she told Anne Edwards, author of *Seeking Balance*. "Without being egotistical, there was nobody on the horizon and I ran more for the party's sake than my own."

Grace, who the Victoria *Times Colonist* called a "faith-healer for still-sick Socreds," lost a by-election by just 42 votes. Within four months, five of the six Socred MLAs had left the party. The sickness was terminal; the Social Credit Party was dead.

But there was life after Social Credit for rebel cabinet minister Grace McCarthy. Sharing her boundless energy and entrepreneurial savvy with an ever-lengthening list of

BC charities and non-profit organizations, Grace is BC's supersaleswoman again, not for a political party this time, but for people in need.

In the early 1990s, Grace's granddaughter was diagnosed with Crohn's disease. The more Grace learned about the debilitating intestinal disorder—its cause is unclear and there is no cure—the more she was determined to help. Working with her daughter and others, Grace founded the CH.I.L.D. Foundation (Children with Intestinal and Liver Disorders). Since 1995, calling on business contacts and former colleagues ("probably the largest network of its kind in the province," according to the *Vancouver Sun*), Grace has helped CH.I.L.D. raise over $15 million for colitis and Crohn's disease research in BC.

Her pathfinding achievements as one of just six women elected to provincial office during W.A.C. Bennett's 22 years as premier, her many imaginative efforts on behalf of BC's economy during the 1970s and 1980s, and her more recent philanthropic commitments have earned Grace a host of awards and recognitions. Among the honours bestowed upon her are the Order of Canada, recognizing "a lifetime of achievement and merit of a high degree," and the Order of British Columbia, which awards those who have, like Grace, "served with the greatest distinction and excelled in any field of endeavour benefiting the people of the Province or elsewhere."

8

Rebel Singer:
Sarah McLachlan

THE STRUGGLES OF THE FEMALE recording artist aren't new. Speaking of her career-launching hit record, 1950s hitmaker Rosemary Clooney said, "When I recorded 'Come On [-a My House],' I wasn't in a position to choose my material, and if I had been, I might not have had the confidence to do it."

Mary Wilson was a member of the 1960s Motown group The Supremes, one of the bestselling vocal groups in American history. Despite the group's string of hits, Mary noted, "The producers had the clout, and that kept the artists begging. The producers treated us not very kindly."

Not much had changed by the 1970s, according to singer Linda Ronstadt: "I was the only girl on the road so the boys always kind of took charge. They [her backup band, the future Eagles] were working for me, and yet it always seemed like I was working for them."

In the 1980s, Pat Benatar won four consecutive Grammy Awards for best female rock performance, but it wasn't easy. "There weren't a lot of women to emulate, no one female figure, so I took a shot in the dark and tried to figure out a way to do this."

In direct contrast, after 17-year-old Halifax singer Sarah McLachlan decided music was her career path, she experienced no real struggle at all. Sarah didn't find herself on the torturous road that generations of earlier female recording artists had trudged toward their professional destinations. What Sarah McLachlan found on her Nova Scotia doorstep was a career superhighway.

While still a bored student at Halifax's Queen Elizabeth High, Sarah was the lead singer for a band called October Game. Her life-defining offer came at the group's first official concert, opening for Moev, a West Coast techno group. Moev's guitarist, who also happened to be a partner in a fledgling Vancouver recording company, Nettwerk, was captivated by Sarah's charismatic performance and asked her to join his band. Her parents said no, not until she attended art college and spent two years at the Maritime Conservatory of Music, studying classical guitar, piano and voice.

Two years later, Sarah found Nettwerk waiting. She signed a five-record contract as a solo artist and said farewell to Nova Scotia, family and friends. It was that simple:

no tears, no toil, no years of wishin'-and-a-hopin'. The Nettwerk superhighway led Sarah McLachlan straight to a number of sought-after stops, including Recording Opportunities, Stardom, Wealth and one destination that few successful vocal vagabonds ever see, that little hamlet called Artistic Freedom.

Until the late 1960s, only a few established singers got to pick the songs they sang. Record company A&R (Artist and Repertoire) men, the real "hitmakers," told their stars what they would record. Even fewer singers wrote the songs they recorded, until the airwaves became flooded with the Beatles singing Lennon and McCartney compositions. Other "British Invasion" artists followed. Suddenly, everyone was writing.

Even then, new singers recording their own material found it tough to get records released and played. This was the case with Janis Ian's "Society's Child (Baby, I've Been Thinking)," one of 1967's most provocative hits. The 15-year-old unknown recorded her song of interracial teen romance for Atlantic Records, but Atlantic refused to release it. "We took the record and went through 21 companies, but no one would buy it," Janis recalled. "They were all afraid to touch it with the straightforward lyric."

Verve/Folkways finally said yes, the third time around, but many radio stations refused to play the record. "They said the lyrics would alienate their audience, which I thought was pretty stupid," Janis said. Only after she performed her heart-rending composition on a TV special, to instant acclaim, did radio programmers accept the song.

Janis Ian and dozens of other female singer-songwriters had helped pave Sarah's way, and she knew it. Hearing "about artists getting eaten up," even in the comparatively enlightened 1990s, Sarah counted herself "so lucky for Nettwerk to find me and give me that opportunity."

Nettwerk gave her something else, too. Until Sarah lifted her guitar out of the case in Vancouver, the only writing she had done was what she dismissively called "little ditties." (Almost all the songs Sarah sang with October Game were from the boys in the band.) Nettwerk allowed her time to find her muse, her voice and her writing ability, on what Sarah once called "blind faith."

"I can spend four months on a song, leaving it and going back to it," she confessed to Chris Dafoe of the *Globe and Mail*. As Sarah, Nettwerk and her fans were to discover, patience can be an extremely rewarding virtue.

By January 1989, Sarah was telling the *Calgary Herald* she had "wanted to become a musician, be like Kate Bush or Peter Gabriel, have a cult following and make the most amazing music." These were lofty dreams, considering all the faded, jaded wannabes and "shouldabeens" littering the road to singing success.

Two CDs later, with *Touch* (1988) and *Solace* (1991) on their way to gold status, Sarah McLachlan was a certified Canadian singing star, touring most of the first part of 1992 in the US and UK. She returned to Vancouver for a well-deserved rest before writing and recording a third release, eagerly awaited by both Nettwerk and her US label, Arista, as her American breakout.

It had been a long time coming. *Rolling Stone* had finally decided to give Sarah a mention in its "New Faces" column, a move that must have had faithful Canadian fans snickering coast to coast and Nettwerk folks heaving a collective sigh of relief. What was needed now was that new release. Sarah, however, abruptly flew to Asia for another tour.

This tour was not what the music business expected of an up-and-coming star. There were no sound checks, cheering crowds or encores. Instead, there were disease-ravaged children in primitive hospitals and adolescent prostitutes ogled by middle-aged tourists. Sarah McLachlan was on a nine-day filmmaking tour of World Vision projects in Cambodia and Thailand. The experience affected her profoundly. "All these things I've taken for granted all my life, health care, clean water, food, a roof over my head," she told the *Vancouver Sun*, "these kids don't have that, and it was really a shock to my system."

The warp and weft of Thailand's street life found their way into "Ice," one of the new songs on 1993's *Fumbling Towards Ecstasy*: "Tied down to this bed of shame; Tried to move around the pain." Another song, "Possession," had its genesis in the troubling star worship Sarah read into fan emails.

For artists, reaching inside themselves and yanking out revealing personal reflections is not an act of rebellion. Artists are supposed to give their complex feelings expression on stage, canvas, paper or microchip. To be true rebels, artists must defy convention and choose to do what others—even those who revere the artist's integrity—deem unacceptable. As a newly electrified Bob Dylan discovered, reverent fans are often far less accepting of change than other mortals.

While many female artists hacked their way through a jungle of tangled personal agendas, contractual quicksand and poisonous media reaction, "Superhighway Sarah" was bumping up against her own barriers. Back in 1991, she had told the *Globe and Mail* that she didn't care about radio. When concerts were building her initial following, there was some validity to that sentiment. Five years later, Sarah did care about the US radio exposure she wasn't getting. Radio-format rotation excluded back-to-back female vocals, which limited not only her airplay, but that of other female singers.

Sarah told organizers she wanted newcomer Paula Cole to open for her on the *Fumbling Towards Ecstasy* tour. Organizers shook their heads. Potential ticket-buyers wouldn't accept two women on the same bill. A quick glance at the concert calendar told Sarah that the scene was completely male-dominated. Now she understood one reason why.

Sarah had achieved everything she'd wanted and more:

Fumbling Towards Ecstasy had turned platinum, swelling the ranks of her US followers by millions of fans. She had even managed to override the naysayers and add Paula Cole to the tour. However, Sarah's own squabbles proved that industry gender inequity affected all female artists, regardless of their success level. Sarah wasn't exactly struggling, but others were. They needed help.

Sarah could have played it safe. There was no external pressure on her to become a champion of anything at all. Her career circumstances were so sunny, there seemed no desperate need to make news. If Sarah stepped out to help others, it would only be by choice. When that happened, Sarah would become defined as more than a singer. She would become a rebel.

By spring 1996, Sarah probably felt she could use a little help herself. Her sometimes reluctant muse had decided to take an untimely hiatus; her songwriting was going nowhere. Manager Terry McBride suggested that the frustrated singer perform some live shows. She agreed, but only with other women performers, "so that we can support each other, so that we can learn from each other."

Sarah's "girlie goddess tour" of four all-female concerts became a trial run for something more ambitious. The omens were good: the final three dates were all sellouts. A few weeks later, Sarah publicly announced an all-woman concert festival tour for the following summer and gave it a name: Lilith Fair. In Jewish myth, Lilith was Adam's first

Garden of Eden partner. The opinions held by the pre-Eve lovely differed from Adam's. At this point, God was on Adam's side, and Lilith was banished. Despite some angelic counselling, she decided to remain on the dark side, or, as the feminist spin has it, fight for the rights of women.

"An interesting twist to the festival idea," wrote Peter Howell of the *Toronto Star*, in what would become one of the classic understatements of popular music history.

A major all-woman tour was a brand new concept. When asked if they would like to participate, so many new performers came on board that two more stages were added to give artists with limited exposure a rare opportunity to, as Sarah put it, "shine in front of thousands . . . and to have the media attention they might not otherwise get."

Veteran headliner Suzanne Vega gave *Maclean's* readers a personal perspective: "I feel like I'm taking part in something historic, something that's never been done before."

"I've waited 20 years to see this happen," Pat Benatar said, "and it's beyond thrilling."

However, it was the girls-only gender issue that inspired the inevitable spate of "Vulvapolooza" and "Estrofest" nicknames and that had rabid media outlets foaming at the mouth. *Time* magazine's cover (Jewel on the US edition; Sarah on the Canadian one) announced: THE GALS TAKE OVER.

What was portrayed as good news by some media outlets was bad news for others. "Incredibly dorky," groaned Ben Rayner of the *Ottawa Sun*. (Rayner might have looked up the other definition of his chosen put-down, which turns out to be, ironically, "penis.") "It's a bunch of folksy, braless ladies. So what?" he went on. Then, echoing the criticism of other arbiters of taste, Rayner snorted, "They don't even rock." Perhaps Rayner was at the food concession when the Indigo Girls fuzz-toned their way through "Shame on You," Meredith Brooks stomped out "I Need" and Paula Cole shouted "Mississippi."

So much media attention made roots-rocker Ani DiFranco—who had performed in the shadows for so long—decidedly suspicious. Lilith Fair smelled of artistic compromise. "Right away, by the name, you know they aren't pushing the envelope hard enough," DiFranco sniped in *Spin*. "It's not The Rolling Thunder Pussy Review." But why would Sarah want to alienate men?

"If I took every opportunity to spout feminism then, sadly, men would be terrified of the tour," Sarah reasoned. The fair had goals to reach, and "we couldn't have it marginalized." This, Sarah emphasized, was a music festival, "not a political campaign."

Besides, the fair's lineup was "a reflection of my taste," Sarah explained. "These are women I wanted to hear." Despite what could be construed as damn-the-fans egocentricity, it was soon obvious that hundreds of thousands wanted exactly what Sarah wanted. With weeks of dates still to go, *Entertainment Weekly* was declaring, THE WOMEN OF LILITH TOUR ARE NOW SUMMER'S HOT TICKET.

It was an impressive ticket: more than 50 female acts (including Jewel, Suzanne Vega and Paula Cole) rotated through the lineup for 37 shows in 35 North American cities. In the months that followed, media collectively threw up its hands and capitulated. *Rolling Stone* concluded that Lilith Fair had been "last summer's biggest success story." The tour, *Entertainment Weekly* said, "forcefully shoved a number of lessons down the throats of the music industry," including the fact that an all-woman tour could be taken seriously and "attract crowds and make a profit."

But profit was not the big priority. From the outset, Sarah saw the tour as a vehicle for not only helping the performers, but assisting a long list of charities that promoted wellness and learning. Able to finance the tour itself, Nettwerk had initially turned sponsors away; however, when some appeared willing to make charitable donations, Nettwerk and McLachlan reconsidered, but only if sponsors and site vendors met the organizers' requirements. When Tommy Hilfiger wanted to brand the fair, Lilith waved Tommy off. It was a cheeky move. A mere singer—the performer—was rewriting concert rules.

She was also handing out cheques to local charities everywhere the tour went. In Seattle, a women's shelter spokeswoman said its $20,000 Lilith Fair donation would keep the doors open another year. Lilith Fair rolled again in the summers of 1998 and 1999, and when the counting was done, donations totalled over $10 million. Then, unexpectedly,

135

Sarah McLachlan decided that she'd had enough, not just of the female concert franchise she had created, but the whole scene: writing, recording and performing.

Back in 1958, a reporter had screwed up his courage and asked the world's biggest recording star if he would lose his popularity when the US Army called him up. "That's the $64,000 question," Elvis sighed. "I wish I knew."

Fifty years later, a singing star's prolonged absence from studio production or stage, radio and video exposure remains an industry nightmare. Some absences, like Elvis' 18-month army hitch or Gloria Estefan's 11-month bus-crash recovery period, can't be avoided, but few would actually choose to leave it all behind. That's putting yourself ahead of your obligation to fans and your record label—just like a rebel.

During her years away, Sarah, in typical style, did what she wanted to do. She spent time with her dying mother and had a baby. She created a musical education foundation and initiated its pilot project, a music school for Vancouver inner-city kids. She also contributed a song to the soundtrack of *Toy Story* and released a live-performance CD, *Mirrorball*.

When Sarah decided to return to the studio and stage, her fans were waiting. But back in 1999, who could have predicted that would happen? Once again, Sarah McLachlan led the way. If it was okay for Sarah to step back, maybe other Lilith alumni could, too. Paula Cole, "running furiously on the same hamster wheel," just "walked away," as the *Los Angeles Times* put it. Her manager warned her that she would never get another record deal. He was wrong—it was just eight years between releases, that's all. Suzanne Vega took five years between releases, longer than some other singers' entire careers.

"I'm just thrilled you're still here," Sarah humbly told the crowds watching her perform songs new and old in 2004. The three-time Grammy Award winner was back with a vengeance, winning yet another Grammy nomination for *Afterglow* (best pop vocal album) and two more Canadian Juno Awards for songwriter and pop album of the year. Definitely back and definitely not forgotten, pop-music rebel Sarah McLachlan would, once again, make music on her own terms.

In 2009, Sarah and her Lilith Fair co-founders decided to stage a revival of the headline-grabbing concert festival that had stunned the music industry and drawn hundreds of thousands of fans over three consecutive summers. The news undoubtedly raised some eyebrows. The three-year Lilith Fair had last toured 11 years before. Time had moved on. Surely fans had moved on, as well. If that was true, it didn't matter, because Sarah and Lilith had moved on, too, at least, electronically.

Ironically, it was the old rationale—a summertime travelling introduction to fresh female talents—that now attracted a host of young online-savvy music fans. Avoiding traditional media outlets, Lilith co-founder Terry McBride sent them Sarah's news directly, in an April 2009 Twitter post: "Lilith Fair 2010 here we come!!" Months of strategic "announcements" designed to build the "buzz" followed on Lilith's own website.

Moreover, Lilith Fair 2010 boasted a partnership that allowed the fair to search out and audition new talent via the internet months before the roster of performers was complete and the festival's locations were finalized. Another partnership helped create the non-profit "i4c" Foundation, with its own on-site festival village, where fans would be encouraged to make donations "for a better tomorrow," through support for innovative triple-bottom-line (people, planet and profit) enterprises.

Nor would those unable to see Lilith entertainers in person be left out. Lilith organizers shook hands with ABC Entertainment Group management to put festival performances online and on TV.

The rebel woman who continued to make music and deliver music on her own terms was now using that music to change the world—on her own terms.

Bibliography

Baird, Irene. "Sidown, Brother, Sidown!" *C.C. Free Press*, July 16, 1973.

_____. *Waste Heritage*. Ottawa: University of Ottawa Press, 2007.

Childerhose, Buffy. *From Lilith to Lilith Fair*. Vancouver: Madrigal Press Ltd., 1998.

Clark, Robert A. "Walker, Mary Richardson (1811–1897)." Essay 7204. HistoryLink: The Free Online Encyclopedia of Washington State History. www.historylink.org.

Drent, Jan. "Labour and the Unions in a Wartime Essential Industry: Shipyard Workers in BC, 1939–1945." Northern Mariner 6 (October 1996): 47–64.

Duniway, Abigail Scott. *Path Breaking: An Autobiographical History of the Equal Suffrage Movement in Pacific Coast States*. New York: Krawus Reprint Co., 1971.

Edwards, Anne. *Seeking Balance: Conversations with BC Women in Politics*. Halfmoon Bay, BC: Caitlin Press, 2008.

Emery, Parris. *America's Atomic Sweetheart: A Composite Biographical Profile of Washington's Maverick Lady Governor, Dixy Lee Ray*. Seattle: Century Publishing Company, 1978.

Fitzgerald, Judith. *Building a Mystery: The Story of Sarah McLachlan and Lilith Fair*. Kingston: Quarry Press Inc., 2000.

Guzzo, Louis. *Is It True What They Say About Dixy? A Biography of Dixy Lee Ray*. Mercer Island, WA: The Writing Works, 1980.

Horn, Michiel. "Transient Men in the Depression." *Canadian Forum* (October 1974): 36–38.

Kesselman, Amy. *Fleeting Opportunities: Women Shipyard Workers in Portland and Vancouver during World War II and Reconversion.* Albany: State University of New York Press, 1990.

Light, Beth and Ruth Roach Pierson, eds. *No Easy Road: Women in Canada 1920s to 1960s.* Toronto: New Hogtown Press, 1990.

Mason, Gary and Keith Baldrey. *Fantasyland: Inside the Reign of Bill Vander Zalm.* Toronto: McGraw-Hill Ryerson, 1989.

McKee, Ruth K. *Mary Richardson Walker: Her Book. The Third White Woman to Cross the Rockies.* Caldwell, ID: The Caxton Printers, 1945.

Moynihan, Ruth Barnes. *Rebel for Rights: Abigail Scott Duniway.* New Haven, CT: Yale University Press, 1983.

Oregon Historical Society. *Northwest Women's History Project.* Portland, 1981.

Owens-Adair, Bethenia. *Dr. Owens-Adair: Some of Her Life Experiences.* Portland: Mann & Beach, 1923.

Persky, Stan. *Fantasy Government: Bill Vander Zalm and the Future of Social Credit.* Vancouver: New Star Books, 1989.

_____. *Son of Socred: Has Bill Bennett's Government Gotten B.C. Moving Again?* Vancouver: New Star Books, 1979.

Ray, Dixy Lee. *Environmental Overkill: Whatever Happened to Common Sense?* With Louis Guzzo. Washington, DC: Regnery Gateway, 1993.

_____. *Trashing the Planet; How Science Can Help Us Deal with Acid Rain, Depletion of the Ozone, and Nuclear Waste (Among Other Things).* With Louis Guzzo. Washington, DC: Regnery Gateway, 1990.

Shein, Debra. *Abigail Scott Duniway.* Boise, ID: Boise State University, 2002.

Smith, Joe. *Off the Record: An Oral History of Popular Music.* Edited by Mitchell Fink. New York: Warner Books, Inc., 1988.

Wright, Richard Thomas. *Overlanders: The Epic Cross-Canada Treks for Gold, 1858–1862.* Williams Lake, BC: Winter Quarters Press, 2000.

Index

Acknowledgements

Dozens of books, newspapers and online documents were consulted during the research and writing of *Rebel Women of the West Coast*. The author is grateful to these historians and writers, many of whom are listed in the bibliography.

Appreciation is extended to those who took the time to advise the author: former Dixy Lee Ray media consultant Lou Guzzo; Laurie Lee, Viewer Services, KCTS 9, for details of Ray's *Animals of the Seashore* broadcasts; Jean M. Ward, Professor Emerita at Oregon's Lewis & Clark College, for historical context and personal details of Bethenia Owens-Adair; and former BC premier Bill Vander Zalm, for his reminiscences of cabinet minister Grace McCarthy and the political issues in the 1970s and 1980s.

A special thanks to University of Ottawa Press, which graciously allowed the author the privilege of quoting extensively from Irene Baird's *Waste Heritage*.

Canadians owe a debt of gratitude to BC author Richard Thomas Wright, whose exhaustively researched book *Overlanders* offers the most comprehensive overview of this fascinating group of 19th-century pioneers.

British Columbians owe the same debt to Stan Persky, whose books *Son of Socred*, *Bennett II* and *Fantasy Government* chronicle a half-century of tumultuous BC politics with ironic insight and great good humour.

About the Author

Author and freelance journalist Rich Mole has been a broadcaster, communications consultant and the president of a successful Vancouver Island advertising agency.

Rich is the author of numerous books, including *Murder and Mystery in the Yukon, Rebel Women of the Gold Rush, Gold Fever* and *The Chilcotin War.* Other non-fiction titles include *Christmas in British Columbia, Christmas in the Prairies* and the hockey histories *Great Stanley Cup Victories* and *Against All Odds,* the story of the Edmonton Oilers.

Rich now lives in Calgary, where he is currently at work on a second novel. He can be reached at ramole@telus.net.